A HERETIC'S MANIFESTO

A HERETIC'S MANIFESTO

Essays on the Unsayable

Brendan O'Neill

Connor Court Publishing

Australian Edition with Introduction

Published by Connor Court Publishing Pty Ltd, 2023.

PO Box 7257

Redland Bay, Queensland, 4165

www.connorcourtpublishing.com.au

First published in 2023 by Spiked Ltd

in association with
London Publishing Partnership

Spiked Ltd
c/o Sierra Quebec Bravo
7th Floor, 77 Marsh Wall
London E14 9SH
www.spiked-online.com

ISBN: 9781922815774 (paperback)

Cover design: Alex Dale

Printed in Australia

CONTENTS

AUSTRALIAN INTRODUCTION

Ten years ago I gave a speech in Sydney about the nanny state. I started off by saying I hate the phrase 'the nanny state' because it's too quaint. Too coy. It doesn't capture what we're up against.

The problem we face today is not some comically overzealous Mary Poppins-style officials always telling us off for necking too much booze or eating 'bad' food. It's an unhinged state that has lost all sense of which areas of life it is appropriate for the authorities to intervene in and which areas of life they should leave well alone.

Forget killjoyism, I said – it's this killing of the Enlightenment-era belief that the citizen should be left to his own devices we should be worried about. The state's non-stop nagging about our eating habits, drinking, smoking, parenting style, speech and even thought has more in common with the Inquisition than with Mary Poppins, I put it to the good Sydneysiders who came to hear me speak.

Fast forward to 2023 and now I feel the same about the phrase 'cancel culture'. Don't get me wrong: it's a useful phrase. It's witty, alliterative. And people understand it. The chattering classes love to say cancel culture is a myth, but people out there know that isn't true. They know cancellation for wrongthink is real. They know there's a privileged layer in society that will demonise, blacklist and damn as a social leper anyone who dares to dissent from the new orthodoxies on gender, identity, race and all the rest.

But I now think 'cancel culture', like 'nanny state', just doesn't cut it as a description of the tyranny of our times. It's too cute. It's like referring to the Inquisition as 'information management' or to Salem as 'accountability culture'. It's another euphemism that risks minimising rather than illuminating the depth of intolerance of the early 21st century.

Just imagine if, 10 years ago, someone had told you that in the future a woman would be hounded out of the Liberal Party for believing that people with penises are men, not women. You'd have thought them mad. Liberals don't punish people for what they think, and they certainly don't punish people for thinking biology is real, you might have protested.

Well, it happened. Moira Deeming was unceremoniously suspended by the Victorian Liberals for the moral error of attending a Let Women Speak rally – a gathering of women who believe, correctly, that 'transwomen' are men and should stay out of women-only spaces.

Deeming is treated like a witch. On *Q+A* the non-binary activist Deni Todorovic said of her: 'Doll… stay at home.' This misogynistic statement, this stern male censure of a supposedly uppity woman, won whoops and cheers from the audience. Again, imagine if someone had told you a decade ago that, soon, blokes who tell birds to stay indoors will be celebrated on ABC's prime political show. You'd have laughed.

This is how swiftly the new intolerance has taken hold. Things that were perfectly sayable just a few years ago are unsayable now.

Heresy-hunting is back. Sure, no stakes are being assembled for the burning of witches. But the atmosphere of the witch-hunt, the vibe of it, lives and breathes today as it did 500 years ago.

The new heretics are JK Rowling, gender-critical feminists, climate-change sceptics, populists, un-PC comics, anyone who utters a peep of criticism of Islam. An entire new grammar of censorship has been fashioned to paint these heretics as unfit for public life. They're damned as transphobes, Islamophobes, bigots, racists, deniers.

That last slur, typically hurled at those who question the cranky claim that climate change is an extinction-level event, comes directly from the Inquisition. Just as those who queried the truth of the Bible were branded 'deniers' and punished with fire, now those who question the End Times predictions of the Cult of Greta Thunberg are called 'deniers' and punished with ostracism.

Australia is teeming with such eco-heretics, apparently. 'The number of climate deniers in Australia is more than double the global average', howled a headline a few years ago. No doubt Australia is meant to feel ashamed of its legion 'deniers' (I prefer to call them sceptics). I think it should take pride in them. For it suggests that DH Lawrence's observation of Oz still holds true. Namely, that it shook off England's 'aristocratic principle' that the 'superior classes' must instruct the little people on how to think and behave, and instead believes that ordinary people should be 'the only source of authority'. To the fury of the global guardians of neo-orthodoxy, Australia often hums and crackles with dissent.

The new war on heresy mimics the old terrifyingly well. As my good friend Bill Leak – peace be upon him – once said: 'If you're found guilty of heresy against the new religion [of political correctness], its perpetually offended and outraged adherents respond with the same sort of savagery that once drove Christians to burn witches at the stake and now drives Islamists to acts of mass murder.'

Against this suffocating culture, we urgently need to restate the civilisational value of free thought. Heresy is the 'perpetual New World, the unknown sea, toward which the brave all sail', said Robert G Ingersoll, the great American defender of liberty. 'Heresy is a cradle; orthodoxy, a coffin', he wrote. Well, now, let us rise from the coffin of samethink and say clearly what we believe to be true. It's the only way to break the stranglehold the new Torquemadas have over our lives and minds. Heretics, assemble.

INTRODUCTION

Lately, I have found myself agreeing with the people who say cancel culture is a myth. Not because I share in their denialism about the mortal threat free speech faces today. Not because I think they're right to be so blasé about the march of intolerance through the institutions. Not because, like many of them, I have succumbed to the cheap thrill of political correctness, to that 'hideous ecstasy of fear and vindictiveness', to use Orwell's words, that always attends attempted mob shutdowns of offensive speech.

No, it's because that phrase – cancel culture – just doesn't cut it. It just doesn't capture what we're up against. It's too soft. Too quaint. Cute, almost. It's like referring to the Inquisition as information management or to Salem as accountability culture. It's too euphemistic. And like all euphemisms, with their embarrassment at bluntness, their discomfort with the unpleasantries of truth, it disguises more than it illuminates. That phrase makes it sound like we are experiencing a mere inconvenience – the bloody drag of occasional cancellation – when in truth we are living through one of the gravest reversals of free thought and of Enlightenment itself of modern times. Sorry to say it so uneuphemistically.

I get the attraction of the phrase 'cancel culture'. It's compact, it's alliterative, it's amusing, it does the job. 'Cancel' means the decision that something will not take place. 'Culture' means the customs of a particular people or society. Yes, that will do – it is now the custom of our society to ensure that the utterance of a disagreeable or offensive thought shall not take place. Accurate and neat.

And yet, not enough. The problem today is not those cancellations of high-profile people we read about in the papers every other week. Nor is it those woke agitators possessed of blue hair and red faces who jealously guard the gates of the modern academy from barbarians who think differently to them. Cursed snowflakes! No, there's more to it than that. So much more.

Beyond cancellation, or perhaps before cancellation, there's our society's colossal loss of faith in freedom. Its turn against reason. Its rejection of the modern idea that people have the capacity to work out for themselves what is right and what is wrong. Its abdication of the burdens of truth-seeking and logic, to such an extent that you can now be expelled from polite society for saying men are men. For saying that if you have a penis, you are not a woman. The hysteria that dictates the punishment of people for saying sex is real, that biology exists, is not captured in the idiosyncratic term 'cancel culture'. We need new terms to describe this post-science, post-truth top-down rage against anyone who dares to give voice to ideas which, around seven years ago, would have been considered completely uncontroversial.

It is the thesis of this short book that the constant churn of political correctness – or cancel culture or wokeness or intolerance or whatever we're calling it – represents not just an over-the-top clampdown on speech, but a crisis of Enlightenment. Every enlightened idea – science is real, race is not, women should have rights, freedom is good, reason is the best tool for making sense of our world – risks being crushed under the forever spinning wheel of correct thought. Our curse is not just to bear witness to the intermittent silencing of controversial commentators, but to watch as liberty, objectivity, democracy, equality and the other great gains of the modern era are sacrificed one by one at the altar of new orthodoxies that pose, so falsely, as progressive thought.

We are living through a war on heresy. No stakes are being assembled for the burning of witches, sure. No pillories are being constructed so that we might throw tomatoes and insults at the eccentric and unorthodox. And yet, the atmosphere of the witch-hunt, the vibe of it, lives and breathes today as it did 500 years ago. The new heretics are JK Rowling, gender-critical feminists, populists, climate-change 'deniers', people who bristle at the diktats issued by the learned as to how we should think and how we should speak. You won't be set on fire, no, but your life will be, your career will be.

We underestimate the importance and wonder of heresy at our peril. Heresy is freedom. Let us heed the words of Robert G Ingersoll, the great 19th-century American defender of free thought: 'Heresy is the eternal dawn, the morning star, the glittering herald of the day. Heresy is the last and best thought. It is the perpetual New World, the unknown sea, toward which the brave all sail. It is the eternal horizon of progress. Heresy extends the hospitalities of the brain to a new thought. Heresy is a cradle; orthodoxy, a coffin.'

Heresy is the perpetual New World. There it is. The invitation to daring that heresy issues to us all. Rarely has the need of heresy been as great as it is right now. In this book you will find not just analysis of the suffocating orthodoxies of our right-thinking era, but also the furious inspirations of heretical thought. They can cancel our speeches, our jobs, our respectability, sometimes even our rights, but they cannot cancel this – the freedom of every person to think and believe as he sees fit. Heresy always finds a way.

1

HER PENIS

We need to talk about her penis. Not about any specific individual's private parts. That would be weird. No, we need to talk about the union of those two words. The smashing together of the female pronoun and the noun for the male genital organ. *Her penis.* Nothing better captures the irrationalism of our age, and also the slippery authoritarianism of it, than the fact that this nonsensical phrase is frequently uttered, and as much in the respectable press as in the gender Bedlam of internet discussion forums. If anyone tries to tell you the culture war is a myth, show them her penis.

Her penis is everywhere. It regularly pops up in news reports. You'll see it in *The Times* and on the BBC. It's inescapable. 'Ex-soldier exposed her penis and used wheelie bin as sex toy in public', said a headline in *Metro* in April 2022.[1] 'A Glasgow-born sex offender has admitted exposing her penis', said the *Daily Record* on that same story.[2] *Teesside Live*, which covers Middlesbrough, the part of the UK in which this mammalistic anomaly reportedly whipped out her phallus, went all out. 'Teesside woman accused of exposing penis', its headline declared. 'She is charged with committing a public nuisance by indecently exposing her penis to other members of the public, while masturbating from a property window', readers were informed.[3] Readers, I'm sure, who will have been more startled by the news that there exists a woman with a penis than by the claims that she flashed it at unsuspecting passers-by.

Speaking of flashing, the *Daily Mail* informed us in September 2021 that an individual 'exposed her penis' at Wi Spa, a spa in Los

Angeles.[4] What's more, 'her penis' was 'partially erect' at the time. A woman with a boner? More proof that there's nothing men can do that women can't. In September 2022, the *Mail* reported on allegations that American college swimmer Lia Thomas 'took out her penis' in the women's locker room.[5] In 2018, the *Daily Mirror* published a hagiographic piece about a 'woman who spent thousands of pounds transforming her body', but who decided to 'keep her penis'.[6] She then 'realis[ed] that she is a lesbian'. Is anyone else confused? The media are meant to report facts, clearly and pithily, but that *Mirror* piece left me bewildered. A woman with a penis who has sex with other women? You mean a straight man?

Her penis even makes an appearance in institutions of longstanding repute. The British Film Institute published a review of the 2018 Belgian film, *Girl*, in which it said one of the characters 'tucks her penis between her legs with tape during strenuous ballet rehearsals'.[7] A few years back, the BBC reported on the 'transgender woman [who] says she was held at an airport because her penis showed up as an "anomaly" when she was going through security'.[8] I bet it did. Even *The Times*, the newspaper of record, occasionally features her penis. Its review of trans activist Grace Lavery's memoir, *Please Miss: A Heartbreaking Work of Staggering Penis*, referred to 'her penis'.[9] The author of that review at least had enough of a grip on reality, however feeble, to say 'her penis' is 'a phrase I pray I never get used to writing'. Though this does raise the question of why it was written in the first place. Why Britain's most esteemed newspaper, renowned for its publication of vital information, would publish those two little words which, when placed in succession, become misleading and outright fraudulent: *her penis.*

At times, the appearance of her penis isn't just strange or spurious – it's sinister. Consider the trial of Karen White. White is a man, and a rapist, and a paedophile. Despite this, he was sent, following his conviction for his grim crimes, to a women's prison: HMP New Hall in West Yorkshire. He says he's a woman and the prison estate believes him. There, he sexually assaulted two inmates.[10] At his trial for those assaults the prosecuting lawyer described White's approach of one of the female inmates as follows: 'Her penis was erect and sticking out the top of her trousers.'[11] *Her penis. Her trousers.* Even the violent, rapacious tormentors of women are afforded the titles 'she' and 'her' if that is what they desire. Even the assaulters of females are addressed in feminine terms, as they please. They rape you *and* they get your pronouns. Even in a courtroom, where all swear to speak the truth, that strangulated act of Newspeak – *her penis* – is spoken, and taken seriously.

Her penis is all the rage with the police, too. At the end of 2021, Police Scotland said rapes would be recorded as having been committed by women 'where a person, born male but who identifies as a female... commits [the] rape'.[12] In 2019, Freedom of Information requests were submitted to UK police forces regarding their attitude towards men who identify as women. Sixteen forces said they recorded data according to the accused's self-declared gender rather than his or her birth sex, and eight of those forces said they do this even when the crime in question is rape.[13] Britain's National Police Chiefs Council likewise advised that people should be referred to by their self-identified gender rather than their natal sex.[14] So there will be cops in the UK who say her penis. Who say that an individual used her penis to rape a woman. Who lie even as they seek the truth.

Her penis. Say those two words to yourself. They are a falsehood, aren't they? Certainly all the examples cited above were lies masquerading as news. That 'woman' in Teesside who exposed 'her penis' and wanked it in front of strangers – that was a man called Andrew McNab who now goes by the name Chloe Thompson. That person who allegedly exposed 'her' partially erect penis in a spa in Los Angeles – that was a man called Darren Agee Merager, who reportedly has a history of indecent exposure.[15] Swimmer Lia Thomas, who allegedly 'took out her penis' in the women's changing room – that was a man whose original name was Will Thomas, who went from being an average male US college swimmer to being among the top female college swimmers when he decided to become Lia. That prisoner, Karen White, who approached a fellow inmate with 'her penis' sticking out of the top of 'her trousers' – that is a man called Stephen Terence Wood whose crimes include indecently assaulting two boys aged nine and 12 and raping a pregnant woman.[16]

His penis, his penis, his penis. That's the phrase you're looking for. 'His' is the only possessive pronoun that should ever appear before the word penis. But of course we are dealing with more than a failure of grammar here. A refresher course on English will not be enough to fix the strange 21st-century tendency of both the mainstream media and the judicial system to say 'her penis'. No, this is a failure of reason. It's a failure of rationalism. That 'her penis' appears everywhere now – from *The Times* to court proceedings to the deliberations of police forces investigating allegations of rape – speaks to the modern era's abandonment of reality and its acquiesence to a new form of cultural authoritarianism that demands the sanctification of people's subjective delusions over and above objective truth. The untruth of 'her penis' is reflective of the legion untruths we are all forced to labour under in this era of linguistic and moral tyranny.

Here's why her penis matters. First, because the widespread use of that false couplet of words shatters the claim made by some commentators that wokeness is a minority pursuit. That political correctness – the manipulation of language so that it accords with the worldview of a new cadre of ideologues – is not as ubiquitous as some observers claim. That's the strange thing about the early 21st century: we're living through both a culture war and some serious culture-war denialism. Often, the people who are most zealous about purging the old, reason-based ways of understanding the world, and replacing them with new forms of correct-think that insist, among other things, that women can have penises, will flat-out deny that they are doing any such thing. Talk about gaslighting. Political correctness is a 'toxic myth' put about by 'wealthy conservatives', says one very politically correct writer.[17] The idea that there are ranks of thoughtpolice, 'all drunk with power, purging the old order', is built on 'lies', she says. 'The truth about "political correctness" is that it doesn't actually exist', claims *Vox* magazine.[18]

Her penis is a battering ram against such flagrant denialism. Her penis intrudes on these deceitful narratives and exposes their fundamental falseness. For if PC 'doesn't actually exist', if wokeness is a crusade taking place only in the fever dreams of paranoid conservatives, then why is her penis everywhere? How have those two words become part of common parlance? Her penis matters because that tiny phrase and huge falsehood confirms just how insidious the overhaul of speech and thought has become in our era. How, by stealth, mainstream society has come to be convinced that sex is irrelevant, language can be altered at will and truth is subordinate to feeling. You say 'her penis', but I hear all of that.

The infiltration of 'her penis' into the commentary and even *thought* of every institution, from the media to the justice system, demonstrates how successful political correctness's vanquishing of reason has been. 'Her penis', the press and the authorities say, as if it's nothing, as if it's normal, as if those two words, when put side by side, are not an abomination against nature and truth. Newspeak clearly comes naturally to the new elites.

Even the political class has succumbed to the cult of her penis. '[Some] women were born with penises', says UK Labour Party MP Stella Creasy.[19] Labour leader Keir Starmer no doubt thinks himself a saner, more in-touch voice than Ms Creasy when he says 'the vast majority of women… don't have a penis',[20] but of course that is indistinguishable from what Creasy said. Starmer clearly also believes that some women have penises; that there are people out there in full possession of a cock and balls who are literally women. This post-truth derangement infects the American establishment, too. President Biden has not, to my knowledge, uttered that perfidious phrase 'her penis', but he unquestionably believes you can be a 'her' and have a penis. The White House is infused with the transgender ideology. Biden says trans people are 'made in [the] image of God'. Cosplaying as Churchill – though replacing the Nazis Churchill was talking about with those modern-day fascists who outrageously believe in biological sex – Biden said he would fight for trans rights 'in the classroom, on the playing field, at work, in our military, and our housing and healthcare systems'.[21] He called on the parents of America to '[affirm] your child's identity'. That is, if your boy, your son, says he's a girl, accept it, believe it, repeat it. It's no longer him, it's her. Her identity, her life, *her penis*.

'Her penis' stretches across the Western world. It's the utterance that lays bare the insanity of our times. This is the other reason her penis matters – it is symptomatic of the cultural despotism plaguing Anglo-American society. There is now a palpable if sometimes imperceptible pressure not only to say things like 'her penis', but also to *believe* them; to believe that this biological male before you, with his XY chromosomes, his broken voice, *his penis*, is in fact a woman. 'Some women have penises – get over it', as the favoured slogan of some trans activists puts it.[22] Get over biology, in other words. Get over reality. Submit, instead, to the post-truth ideology subscribed to by police forces, politicians, governments and the media which holds that a person with a penis can be a woman and that biological truth, science itself, is passé.

Consider the Orwellian consequences of her penis. Or, rather, of the culture war on nature and reason that that two-word fiction is an expression of. The transgender ideology is central to the worldview of the new elites. And with its twisting of language, its disdain for biological fact, and its inculcating of a new generation with the lie that one's sex is a matter of choice, it's an ideology that feels like a real-life version of Big Brother. In *Nineteen Eighty-Four*, one of Winston Smith's jobs at the Ministry of Truth is to revise old newspaper articles so that their content better accords with Party propaganda. News itself is made subservient to the ideological outlook of the ruling elite. This is happening for real right now. Those reports claiming a 'woman' flashed 'her penis' and a 'woman' assaulted two other women while 'her penis was erect and sticking out the top of her trousers' were not really news – they were propaganda. The truth – that these things were done by men, by *his penis* – was subjugated to the media elites' supposedly higher aim, higher than truth itself, to promote the credo of genderfluidity.

One of the most egregious examples of the media's devotion to ideology leading directly to misinformation appeared in the *New York Times*. Yes, even the Old Gray Lady accepts the idea that a man becomes a lady simply by saying he is such. In March 2022, the *NYT* reported on an '83-year-old Brooklyn woman' who was suspected of murdering and decapitating a 68-year-old woman.[23] Apparently, this elderly lady had killed women before. The headline to the *NYT*'s report said: 'She killed two women. At 83, she is charged with dismembering a third.' The BBC covered this same strange tale of an old woman allegedly cutting off another woman's head. Cops 'searched her apartment', the Beeb said, wherein they found 'a human head'.[24] Her apartment. It was a falsehood. Yet another. In the very last line of that BBC report we learn that this 83-year-old killer of women is someone who 'identifies as a transgender woman'. So, a man. Deep into the *NYT*'s piece it is revealed that the 83-year-old 'was listed as male in earlier court records but now identifies as a woman'. So, a man. 'Her apartment', 'she is charged', 'she killed' two women in the past – these were lies, essentially; fabrications underpinned by an allegiance to the transgender ideology so intense that respecting the preferred pronouns of a male killer of women comes to take precedence over telling the truth about the women's experiences. Their experiences in this case being that they were murdered by a man, one Harvey Marcelin, in *his* apartment, by *his* hands, to sate *his* evil urge to harm women.

The cult of 'her penis' interferes not only with media reporting on crimes, but also with the official recording of crimes. As we have seen, some police forces in the UK log even rapes as having been committed by women if the male culprit identifies as female. 'Police forces let rapists record their gender as female', as a report in *The Sunday Times* said.[25] This undoes the very meaning of rape, which in English and Welsh law is defined as an offence in which a person 'intentionally penetrates the vagina, anus or mouth of another person with his penis', where that other person 'does not consent to the penetration'. *His penis*. It's there in the democratically made law. And yet in practice – in courtrooms, in police stations, in the press – *her penis* is substituted where the rapist is under the delusion that he is a woman. It is a deeply disturbed society that considers validating evil men's hallucinatory identities to be more important than establishing the truth. As one critical media report said, both society and the individual lose out when gender fantasy is elevated above biological reality in the discussion and punishment of crime. Such an approach will 'skew statistics about men's sexual violence against women and further traumatise victims of rape who could be forced in evidence to talk about "her penis" in relation to their rapist'.[26]

Her penis. There it is again. Words even rape victims might have to utter. For these women, that phrase is not only daft, not merely a falsehood – it is also a grave assault on their right to tell the truth about their own experiences. To those who say political correctness is a myth, whipped up by aggrieved old white men, kindly explain how we have arrived at a situation where a victim of sexual assault might be compelled to say 'her penis' about the man who assaulted her? First she's forced by a man to engage in sexual activity; then she's forced by cultural diktat to respect that man's gender delusions. Compelled to have sex, then compelled to lie in order to flatter the fantasies of her attacker. Political correctness now enjoys dominion not only over truth and law, but also over human decency itself.

Compulsion – that's the key thing here. We are all compelled, by various means, to use preferred pronouns, to refer to men as 'she', to accept that sex can be changed, to use post-sex terms like 'individuals with a cervix' and 'chestfeeding'. One of the great heresies of our time is to say that men are men and women are women. Biology is heresy now. GK Chesterton saw this coming. 'We shall soon be in a world', he said, 'in which people will persecute the heresy of calling a triangle a three-sided figure'.[27] We're now in that world. If a triangle identifies as a square, surely it's a square. The *New York Times* would call it a square. The BBC would, too.

In 2017, CNN ran an advertising campaign targeting Donald Trump's 'post-truth' way of thinking. The ad featured a photo of an apple. 'This is an apple', the text said. 'Some people might try and tell you that it's a banana. They might scream banana, banana, banana over and over and over again. They might put BANANA in all caps. You might even start to believe that this is a banana. But it's not. This is an apple.'[28] This is the same CNN that criticised JK Rowling for saying women are women. There are also 'trans women', CNN said, who were 'assigned male at birth but identify as women'.[29] It countered Rowling's heretical expression of biological truth with the words of a spokesperson for an LGBTQ charity: 'It's important [that we recognise] very clearly that trans women are women.' So, what if CNN's apple identified as a banana? Would we have to very clearly recognise that it is a banana? It may have been assigned the status of an apple by the person who picked it, but what if somebody else decides it's a banana now? One day people will be 'howled down for saying that two and two make four', said Chesterton. That day has come. We're howled down for saying XY chromosomes and a penis make a man.

The compulsion to use correct speak, and to have correct thought, in relation to sex and gender takes many forms. Some states have considered using the full weight of the law to enforce compliance with gender ideology. In New York state, the Commission on Human Rights (CHR) published legal guidelines suggesting that employers and landlords should be fined if they fail to use a person's preferred pronouns. If any provider of housing or jobs 'intentionally and consistently' ignores an individual's preferred pronouns, even the more eccentric 'neo-pronouns' such as 'ze / hir', he or she should be subjected to fines as high as $250,000, suggested the CHR.[30] Elsewhere, people are 'encouraged' to respect others' pronouns, and sometimes to display their own. The BBC 'encourages' staff to put their pronouns in their email signatures.[31] Capitalist monoliths like Goldman Sachs, Virgin Management and Lloyds likewise 'encourage' ideologically on-message pronoun-use. 'Encourage' is euphemistic here. Compulsion is at play in these cases, too. As the *Wall Street Journal* reports, some employees bow down to the cult of the preferred pronoun 'at their company's urging'.[32] Urge – to try persistently to persuade. It's a polite way of saying compel.

Social or economic ostracism frequently awaits those who refuse to genuflect to the religion of genderfluidity. Tax expert Maya Forstater was dismissed from her job for refusing to believe that men can become women.[33] Barrister Allison Bailey was discriminated against at work for her belief that sex cannot be changed – that is, for her correct understanding of biology.[34] Children's author Gillian Philip was unceremoniously dumped by both her literary agent and her publisher for the speechcrime of expressing solidarity with JK Rowling. For that – for adding the hashtag #IStandWithJKRowling to her Twitter handle – Ms Philip received 'messages threatening to kill and rape' her. Emails were sent to her publishers demanding her sacking. It all 'ended, a day later, with me losing my livelihood', she said.[35] Twenty-four hours is all it takes for those who express the modern equivalent of Chesterton's 'heresy of calling a triangle a three-sided figure' to be threatened with violence, demonised as evil and sacked. And still they say political correctness is a myth.

Whether compliance with gender ideology is being enforced or 'encouraged', whether people are being pressured to believe by legal diktat or by the deranged threats and howls of the Twittermob, the result is the same: a stifling culture of conformism is imposed, and one blasphemes against it at one's peril. 'But it's polite to use people's preferred pronouns and to affirm their identities, so just do it', some say. As comedian Stewart Lee once said of political correctness, it's only 'institutionalised politeness'. This has nothing to do with politeness. It's about submission. It's about forcing people to surrender to new orthodoxies. It's about bringing heretics to heel. It's about making us doubt the light of our own reason and 'encouraging' us to yield instead to the higher wisdom of ruling ideologues who believe an apple is an apple, but a man is not necessarily a man.

Using people's preferred pronouns, dutifully making an utterance like *her penis* – these are not mere acts of niceness but rather are signifiers of subservience to the disrupting ideology of transgenderism. As one feminist writer says, 'pronouns are not neutral'. Rather, preferred pronouns, especially when compelled, are 'highly political'. People who use preferred pronouns are indicating their acceptance of the belief that 'everyone has an inner gender identity, and being described by the pronouns he / him, she / her, they / them, zie / zem, or something else, is an expression of that identity'.[36] But this belief, she continues, that 'each of us has an inner being, a soul which is gendered, contained inside the mortal flesh which has a reproductive sex that may not match that gender', is a 'quasi-religious' one. In being compelled to say she / her about men, to accept that there's an inner gender and an outer sex and sometimes they are mismatched, we are being compelled to convert to a new religion. The religion of genderfluidity. The religion of gendered souls. Such 'encouraged' conversion runs entirely counter to the Enlightenment itself and to the freedom of conscience it promised humankind. We should never be 'compelled by fire and sword to profess certain doctrines', said John Locke.[37] And yet we are now. We're compelled by the threat of social leprosy to profess the doctrine of 'her penis'.

This is where we can glimpse the most pernicious element of political correctness – its assault on our *inner life.* Through the quasi-religion of genderfluidity, the elites demand not only outward compliance with their belief system, but inward acceptance of it, too. For all the talk of 'politeness', it is actually not sufficient, in their eyes, merely to perform allegiance to gender ideology – no, you must imbibe it, fully, into your soul. As one pro-trans writer says, pronoun use is not just about 'conveying respect' for others – it is also about changing one's own nature: 'Mastering correct pronoun usage is a great first step to understanding more about gender identity.'[38] A writer for *Wired* spells it out more starkly. '[G]ender-neutral pronouns can change a culture', he says. Sure, it's good to 'find language that accommodates people's identities', he says – that is, to be 'polite' – but the more important thing in encouraging the use of preferred pronouns is that it can help to 'incept [a] new idea into *everyone*' (my emphasis).[39] 'New language… can become a useful tool for changing how people deal with each other', he says. '[The] one way culture entrains gender ideas is through language itself', he continues. Through the policing of words, we can 'nudge in the direction of change'.

This is an open confession of the Orwellian impulse that underpins gender ideology in particular and political correctness more broadly. It is not about 'institutionalising politeness' – it's about internalising correct thought. Orwell understood very well the relationship between language and thought, and how control of the former permits control of the latter: '[If] thought corrupts language, language can also corrupt thought.'[40] He devoted much of *Nineteen Eighty-Four* to exploring how the exercise of power over what may be said makes it easier to enjoy dominion over what can be thought, over how individuals understand themselves and their place in society. 'Don't you see', says Syme, a lexicographer at the Ministry of Truth, 'that the whole aim of Newspeak is to narrow the range of thought? In the end we shall make thoughtcrime literally impossible, because there will be no words in which to express it.'[41] The real-world version of that fictional effort to overhaul man's inner life through controlling the language he is allowed to use in society is expressed more softly, though no less sinisterly. 'New language… can become a useful tool for changing how people deal with each other', say the Symes of today.[42]

The new elites have accomplished an extraordinary and terrifying amount of social overhaul through their manipulation of the language of sex and gender. No facet of the human experience has been left untouched by their religion of gendered souls. From birth itself to parenthood to the very ability of our societies to use reason to understand and measure themselves – all have been disrupted by the elites' crusade to change how we speak and think about sex.

The phrase 'sex assigned at birth' radically transforms how we view the very creation of human life. This wording is about challenging 'the standardised relationship between one's genitalia at birth and the assignment of one of two fixed gender identities', as one trans writer puts it.[43] In short, the belief of human society since its very beginnings – that sex can be observed upon birth – was wrong. It was bigoted, in fact. In truth, we cannot truly know the sex of a child, and we shouldn't seek to 'assign' one, because sex and gender are things we feel, not things we are. Boys and girls are no longer born; rather, gender-neutral creatures come into existence and we must allow them to discover their gender as they mature. Such thinking is an offence against reason. Some forms of official documentation seem to be moving towards using that disruptor phrase, 'sex assigned at birth'. The UK Census of 2021 considered permitting those 'whose gender is different from their sex registered at birth' to tick whatever sex box they liked, even if it was not 'the same as their birth certificate'.[44] So even discovering the make-up of our society, the facts of our civilisation, is subjugated to the lie of gender subjectivity.

Our understanding of parenthood is being transformed, too. New words like 'birthing parent', in place of mother, and 'chestfeeding', in place of breastfeeding, 'encourage' us to doubt the distinctive, sex-based qualities of mothering and fathering. Even the National

Health Service uses post-sex terminology when referring to mothers. The NHS Norfolk and Suffolk Foundation Trust has used the phrase 'birthing people'.[45] In some educational institutions, students of midwifery are encouraged to use 'gender-neutral' language, such as 'pregnant people'.[46] Words that have extraordinary meaning in community life – specifically, 'mother' – are slowly being erased to avoid offending against the cult of post-sex relativism. Even birth certificates, the means through which a society records the truth about each new citizen, risk falling victim to gender derangement. Legislation passed in Ireland in 2015 allows transgender people to alter their birth certificates – 'a new birth certificate can be issued to show the preferred gender and new name', reported the *Irish Times*.[47] There have been discussions in the UK about bringing in similar changes, though public support for such Orwellian interference with birth certification has fallen sharply. In September 2022, the British Social Attitudes survey found that the proportion of people who support the alteration of birth certificates to validate people's current gender feeling had fallen from 53 per cent to 32 per cent in the previous two years.[48] Many people clearly recognise the irrational and authoritarian implications of allowing truthful information about who has been born to be memory-holed. Allowing the subjective beliefs of people in the present to override the objective recording of events in the past would be extraordinary – a testament to the extent to which political correctness had overpowered reality entirely.

Motherhood downgraded. Biology reimagined as bigotry. News propagandised. A new generation encouraged to feel so unsure about sex and gender that growing numbers of them profess to be gender-neutral and some even submit themselves to the bodily mortification of puberty-blocking drugs and hormonal correction. These are the consequences of the religion of gendered souls. And all of it is an achievement of language. Of compelling us to speak in a certain way, and thus to think in a certain way, too. Through 'encouraging' compliance with new linguistic rules, and punishing as 'transphobia' any deviation from the rules, the elites have managed to disrupt millennia of human belief and to transform how we think about sex, society, ourselves and our relationships with others. Language is indeed a 'useful tool for changing how people deal with each other'. Let us call the cult of 'her penis' what it is – a chilling act of cultural reprogramming through which we are being wrenched from tradition and organic knowledge and forced into a brave new world where what they say is the truth is the truth. A brave new world in which Spinoza's nightmare vision of tyrannical government – where men are turned from 'rational beings into beasts or puppets' – is a step closer. For when we are incited to be unsure of our identities, uncertain even about the meaning of our own births, and always obedient in our thought and speech, we are less free beings than malleable beasts, ripe for interference and correction by the guardians of thought.

Nothing better captures the need for heresy than the disorientations of the gender religion. We now know the price of not speaking back, of letting others instruct us on what we may utter and how we must think. We now know the cost of allowing incursions into our inner lives. Man must be 'master of his own thoughts', said Spinoza. He must never be 'compelled to speak only according to the diktats of the supreme power'. That is the first task of the heretic, then: to resist compulsion. To speak as he sees. To never fear to express the truth. To refuse, at all costs, to say anything as abominable as 'her penis'.

1 Ex-soldier exposed her penis and used wheelie bin as sex toy in public, *Metro*, 12 April 2022

2 Scot flashed penis and used sex toy in public leaving onlookers shocked, *Daily Record*, 18 February 2022

3 Teesside woman accused of exposing penis, using sex toy and masturbating in public, *Teesside Live*, 25 November 2021

4 Registered sex-offender identifying as a woman – who sparked a riot after 'exposing erect penis to young girl in women's section of LA spa' – is CHARGED with indecent exposure… and it's not the first time, *Daily Mail*, 2 September 2021

5 Swimmer who tied NCAA race with Lia Thomas recalls horror when trans athlete 'who is attracted to women' displayed penis in locker room, *Daily Mail*, 15 September 2022

6 Transgender woman says she's happy she kept her penis – 'because she enjoys sex with women more', *Mirror*, 24 March 2018

7 It's winning awards, but *Girl* is no victory for trans representation, Cathy Brennan, British Film Institute, 30 October 2018

8 Transgender woman's penis 'shows up as anomaly' at Orlando airport, BBC News, 24 September 2015

9 *Please Miss: A Heartbreaking Work of Staggering Penis* by Grace Lavery review – a tiresome, taboo-trashing trans memoir, Sarah Ditum, *The Times*, 7 February 2022

10 Female inmate tells of sex assault by trans prisoner, *Law Society Gazette* (Ireland), 18 January 2022

11 Plan to allow rapists to self-identify as women prompts victims' fury, *The Sunday Times*, 26 December 2021

12 Cops to record rapes as committed by woman if male attacker identifies as female, *Scottish Sun*, 11 December 2021

13 UK police record male rapists as female under self-ID policy, Fair Play For Women, 19 January 2021

14 UK police record male rapists as female under self-ID policy, Fair Play For Women, 19 January 2021

15 Wi Spa suspect still at large – has history of indecent exposure and masturbation, *New York Post*, 17 September 2021

16 Transgender prisoner who sexually assaulted inmates jailed for life, *Guardian*, 11 October 2018

17 Generation Grievance: How the Political Correctness Myth Was Born, Nesrine Malik, *Literary Hub*, 11 May 2021

18 The truth about 'political correctness' is that it doesn't actually exist, *Vox*, 28 January 2015

19 Stella Creasy: 'JK Rowling is wrong – a woman can have a penis', *Daily Telegraph*, 27 May 2022

20 Keir Starmer says 'vast majority' of women 'don't have a penis' and need safe spaces, LBC, 6 June 2022

21 Biden says trans people 'made in image of God', parents must 'affirm' identity, *New York Post*, 31 March 2022

22 LGBWithTheT, Twitter, 8 September 2022

23 She Killed Two Women. At 83, She Is Charged With Dismembering a Third, *New York Times*, 10 March 2022

24 Pensioner arrested after dismembered body found, BBC News, 14 March 2022

25 Police forces let rapists record their gender as female, *The Sunday Times*, 20 October 2019

26 Plan to allow rapists to self-identify as women prompts victims' fury, *The Sunday Times*, 26 December 2021

27 *Collected Works: Volume 1: Heretics, Orthodoxy, The Blatchford Controversies*, GK Chesterton, Ignatius (1986)

28 CNN's new 'This is an apple' ad targets Trump, *Vox*, 23 October 2017

29 Gender identity: The difference between gender, sex and other need-to-knows, Kristen Rogers, CNN, 10 June 2020

30 Not using transgender pronouns could get you fined, *New York Post*, 19 May 2016

31 BBC advises all staff to use trans-friendly pronouns, *The Times*, 10 July 2020

32 Why Gender Pronouns Are Becoming a Big Deal at Work, *Wall Street Journal*, 16 September 2021

33 JK Rowling friend Maya Forstater sacked unfairly over trans view, *The Times*, 7 July 2022

34 Allison Bailey: Barrister awarded £22,000 in discrimination case, BBC News, 27 July 2022

35 I've gone from children's author to truck driver – all because I stood up for JK Rowling, *Daily Mail*, 28 September 2022

36 Pronouns: Compulsion and Controversy, *Legal Feminist*, 19 July 2020

37 *Second Treatise of Government and A Letter Concerning Toleration*, John Locke, Oxford World's Classics (2016)

38 Why Pronoun Use Matters, Ariane Resnick, *Very Well Mind*, 3 March 2022

39 Actually, Gender-Neutral Pronouns Can Change a Culture, Adam Rogers, *Wired*, 15 August 2019

40 *Politics and the English Language*, George Orwell, Penguin Modern Classics (2013)

41 *Nineteen Eighty-Four*, George Orwell, Secker & Warburg (1949)

42 Actually, Gender-Neutral Pronouns Can Change a Culture, Adam Rogers, *Wired*, 15 August 2019

43 *The Transgender Issue: An Argument for Justice*, Shon Faye, Allen Lane (2021)

44 Guidance for questions on sex, gender identity and sexual orientation for the 2019 Census Rehearsal for the 2021 Census, Office for National Statistics

45 So much for the crackdown on NHS wokery! Fury as ANOTHER hospital trust starts calling mothers 'birthing people', *Daily Mail*, 29 August 2022

46 Midwifery students to be told how to look after 'pregnant people' and 'birthing parents' rather than 'women' as degree courses adopt more 'inclusive' language, *Daily Mail*, 10 October 2022

47 Law allows transgender people to get updated birth certs, *Irish Times*, 8 September 2015

48 Support falls for trans people to change sex on birth, *The Times*, 22 September 2022

2

WITCH-FINDING

In 1590, in Scotland, an elderly woman named Agnes Sampson was arrested. She was from East Lothian. Earlier in her life she had been a midwife and a healer, but lately she had been living in poverty. She was tried, found guilty and taken to Edinburgh Castle where, on 28 January 1591, she was strangled to death by rope and then burnt at the stake.[1] Her offence? Climate change.

Sampson was charged with stirring up 'contrary winds', among other things. Her persecution stemmed from the troubles of King James VI whose attempts to bring his new wife, Anne of Denmark, to Scotland were continually thwarted by hellish weather. 'Unusual' winds capsized ships of the royal fleets.[2] Twice did Anne's ship have to dock in Norway due to the 'fierce storms'.[3] James, inspired by reports from Denmark of witches being burnt for their supposed part in the frustration of Anne's journey, became convinced of a witches' plot in Scotland, too. He pushed the idea of 'weather magic', where witches use their demonic power to cause 'unusual' storms, hails and fogs to descend on Earth.[4]

The end result was the North Berwick Witch Trials, one of the deadliest episodes of witch-hunting in the history of Great Britain. Taking place a hundred years before the better-known witch-hunts of Salem in Massachusetts, the hysteria in North Berwick involved 150 accusations, copious amounts of torture to extract confessions and 25 deaths.[5] Mrs Sampson's was just one of those deaths. She and many others had been accused not only of the usual witchy things – mysterious healings, issuing curses and so on – but of something else, too. That they had changed the climate. That they had whipped up destructive weather. That they had deployed their malevolence to the end of 'conjur[ing]' terrible storms 'in cahoots with the devil'.[6] For in the words of Danish admiral Peter Munch, who had been tasked with transporting Anne to Scotland, what his ships had encountered was no normal climatic event – no, 'there must be more in [this] matter than the common perversity of winds and weather'.[7]

The women of North Berwick can be seen as among the earliest victims of climate-change hysteria, of that urge to pin the blame for anomalous weather on wicked human beings. And they weren't alone. In Europe between the 1500s and 1700s, climate change was often the charge made against witches. In his 1584 book, *The Discoverie of Witchcraft*, Reginald Scot, an English MP and author, outlined the common view of witches as climate changers. Many believe witches can 'raise haile, tempests, and hurtfull weather', he said, as well as being able to 'inhibit the sunne, and staie both daye and night, changing the one into the other'. Scot was a witch-sceptic. He called for calm during witch-hunts. His view was that weather was a natural, or heavenly, phenomenon, not the plaything of allegedly evil people. '[It] is neither a witch, nor a devil, but glorious God that maketh the thunder', he wrote. 'God maketh the blustering tempests and whirlwinds' as well, he continued.[8] But his plea for reason fell on deaf ears. Too many people were far more enamoured of the view, soon to be promoted by James VI, no less, that a witch could 'rayse stormes and tempestes in the aire'.[9]

Witch-hunts in mid-millennial Europe were inextricably linked with concerns over climate change. This was the era of the Little Ice Age, the period that roughly spanned from 1300 to 1850 during which the Northern Hemisphere experienced exceptionally cold winters.[10] The impact of the Little Ice Age was devastating. The frigid weather violently disrupted harvests in Europe, especially the grain harvest. Following particularly cold periods in the 1500s, it took *180 years* for grain harvests to return to their previous levels.[11] The result, in the words of German historian Philipp Blom, was 'a long-term, continent-wide agricultural crisis'.[12] And this led to a staggering spike in witch-hunts. Blom describes how in northern Europe in particular, 'the accumulation of bad harvests and the constant fear of famine and illness' led to the rise of 'a particularly cruel collective hysteria: witch trials'. Thousands of women, and occasionally men, were burnt for their alleged role in stoking contrary weather, in causing climate change.

For a long time, says Blom, historians wondered why witch persecutions were 'especially cruel' between the years 1588 and 1600 and again between 1620 and 1650. It's because these were the times of the most extreme cold and most dreadful storms, and the evil cause of such climatic calamities had to be found and extinguished. 'Religious tensions certainly played a role [in that period]', he writes, 'but the correlation among extreme weather events, ruined harvests and waves of witch trials asserts itself most forcefully'.[13]

It is no coincidence that around 110,000 witch trials took place in Europe during those most climatically unstable of centuries, with around half of those trials ending in conviction and execution. As the cold, starving peoples of northern Europe knew from the Bible, 'Thou shalt not suffer a witch to live', especially a witch with such power that she can conjure storms in which 'sea and sky became one'.[14] Johann Weyer, the 16th-century Dutch physician who opposed witch-hunting, describes one woman being forced to admit essentially that she had brought about climate change: '[A] poor old woman was driven by torture to confess – as she was just about to be offered to Vulcan's flames – that she had caused the incredible severity of the previous winter (1565), and the extreme cold, and the lasting ice.'[15]

The cries of those tortured women should echo down the ages. Their persecution for the crime of causing contrary weather should give us pause for thought today. For as German historian Wolfgang Behringer convincingly argues, the weather-related witch hysteria of the early modern period shows how perilous it can be to moralise discussions about the climate. A section of European society during the Little Ice Age held witches 'directly responsible for the high frequency of climatic anomalies', he writes. And the 'enormous tensions created in society as a result of the persecution of [those] witches demonstrate how dangerous it is to discuss climatic change under the aspects of morality'.[16]

Alas, it seems likely that this plea not to moralise discussions about climate will fall on 21st-century ears that are as deaf to reason as were those that ignored Reginald Scot's insistence that weather was a heavenly phenomenon, not the devilish handiwork of warped human beings. For today, in our supposedly enlightened era, the rush to blame sinning and selfish individuals for 'contrary winds', or 'weather of mass destruction', as we call it now, is as intense as it was in the Little Ice Age. Weather witch-finding is alive and well.

Sure, we don't threaten to hurl climate changers into 'Vulcan's flames'. We do not 'thrawn' them with rope, inducing a 'pain most grievous', as was done to poor Mrs Sampson.[17] We don't even say the word witch anymore. No, we prefer to speak of 'climate criminals'. 'Thirteen climate criminals who should be in jail', as the headline in a radical magazine put it a few years ago. The list included everyone from Donald Trump to Big Oil CEOs to broadcasters like Jeremy Clarkson. Clarkson's crime was a speechcrime – to suggest climate change is a 'fiction'. For that, he and the other 'real climate offenders' should be imprisoned, we were told.[18]

'The internet is finally turning on celebrity "climate criminals"', chirped a headline in a fashion magazine in July 2022. That piece had a distinctly witch-hunting vibe, arguing that 'it is right to be outraged' about these people 'who are most responsible for the climate crisis'.[19] We must 'stop the climate criminals who are causing the worst emissions', says a writer for the *Guardian*.[20] One left-wing outlet calls for the jailing of 'climate criminals' on the basis that they played a part in conjuring 'floods... fires, heatwaves and other extreme weather events'.[21] These are the new Agnes Sampsons. They're the modern versions of that woman Johann Weyer described as having been compelled by fire to confess to having brought about unusual coldness. That is, they're people accused of using their wickedness to 'rayse stormes'. Only we call them 'criminals' rather than 'witches', and we say 'climate change' rather than 'contrary winds', because we are enlightened now.

There may not be witch trials in the 21st-century West, but there is certainly the *dream* of witch trials. Especially for those who have the temerity to use their tongues to deny the existence of manmade climate change. As one academic study asks: 'Deceitful tongues: is climate-change denial a crime?'[22] This is Biblical language, literally. Right out of Psalms. 'Thou lovest evil more than good; and lying rather than to speak righteousness. Thou lovest all devouring words, O thou deceitful tongue', says Psalms 52:3-4. Now such stern religious condemnation is deployed against questioners of the climate-change thesis. The author of that piece on the 'deceitful tongues' of the modern age – William C Tucker, then an assistant regional counsel to the US Environmental Protection Agency, no less – said such tongues may indeed need to be silenced. For what they say is not only 'morally repugnant', but potentially criminal, too: '[We] cannot allow fraudulent or deceptive speech to paralyse the public debate on a subject no less important than the survival of the human species and the future of the Earth itself.'[23]

In the past, witches, likely including those who were accused of raising 'hurtfull weather', were sometimes fitted with a 'scold's bridle' – a metal contraption that enclosed the head and which contained a muzzle that fitted into the mouth with a spike that would compress the witch's 'vicious tongue'.[24] Now, being more modern, we prefer to propose mere criminal sanctions against those who possess a 'deceitful tongue'.

The tyranny of holding mass witch trials may no longer be possible in our more civilised era, but the fantasy of such tyranny still exists. 'I wonder what sentences judges might hand down at future international criminal tribunals on those who will be partially but directly responsible for millions of deaths from starvation, famine and disease in decades ahead', environmentalist author Mark Lynas once said.[25] Who are the 'those' in that chilling sentence? Climate-change deniers, of course, who will 'one day have to answer for their crimes', according to Lynas.

Paul Krugman of the *New York Times* describes climate-change denial as 'a form of treason – treason against the planet'.[26] The Kennedy Institute of Ethics at Georgetown University openly ponders whether climate-change denial should be criminalised. Yes, 'free speech is one of the most treasured rights in Western democracy', it says in its discussion of a Norwegian professor's suggestion that climate-change denial is a crime, but sometimes we make 'exceptions for points of view which [may be regarded] as particularly destructive and evil'.[27] *Evil.* What a telling word. As clear a confirmation as one could ask for that the discussion of climate change has been hyper-moralised, turned from a practical matter of how to improve our environment into a crusade against the malevolent forces whose deceitful tongues and activities allegedly wreak havoc upon the weather.

Of course, it isn't only powerful 'climate criminals' who are held responsible for contrary weather today – we all are. We are living through a collectivisation of the witch trial, where all human beings, by mere dint of existence, are said to be contributing to climatic instability. Every weather anomaly is now instantly laid at the feet of humanity.

'With raging wildfires, floods and pandemics, it seems like End Times – and it's our own damned fault', said a writer for the *Hill* in July 2021.[28] A *Guardian* account of the IPCC's sixth and most recent assessment report said we now finally have the 'verdict on [the] climate crimes of humanity' – we are 'guilty as hell'.[29] Professor Tim Palmer of Oxford University draws a direct line between man's allegedly sinful behaviour and various floods and fires across the globe. 'If we do not halt our emissions soon, our future climate could well become some kind of hell on Earth', he says.[30] This view of humankind's weather crimes helping to raise hell to the surface echoes the demonology of James VI, who believed witches were induced by 'all the devils in hell' to commit their storm-raising and other offences.[31]

There is a powerful Old Testament overtone to much of the discussion about climate in the 21st century. Fires and floods are viewed as warnings to humankind about its unholy behaviour. Australia's bushfires 'are a warning to the world', said a climate activist in the *Guardian* in January 2020.[32] Fires in Europe in summer 2022 were described by some as an 'apocalypse of heat'.[33] 'Hell is coming', said a *Guardian* headline.[34] This is 'apocalypse now', we were told, and it's a result of our 'living beyond our means', which is 'the greatest sin of all time'.[35] Floods are likewise cited as reprimands from Mother Nature for our sins. Large rainfalls in the UK in 2007 were described by one green businessman as 'the drumbeat of disaster that heralds global warming'. It feels as though 'behind the gathering clouds the hand of God is busy, writing more bills [for humankind]', he said.[36] Mark Lynas has also described weather anomalies as god-like chastisements of industrious mankind. He said of floods that Poseidon is clearly 'angered by arrogant affronts from mere mortals like us': 'We have woken him from a thousand-year slumber and this time his wrath will know no bounds.'[37]

This idea that weather has a punishing intent, that it is violent payback for the 'affronts' of mankind, also echoes the more hysterical moments of the Little Ice Age. As Philipp Blom documents, alongside singling out covens of witches as the harbingers of climatic mayhem, religious figures also presented contrary weather as an expression of divine 'displeasure'. 'Every earthquake, every volcanic eruption and every storm was interpreted as… a punishment for human wickedness', writes Blom.[38] A 'direct causal link between bad behaviour and bad harvests' was frequently made. Indeed, in the 1500s and 1600s, 'weather sermons became a minor literary genre of their own', he says. One particularly skilled practitioner of the 'weather sermon' was Johann Georg Sigwart, a German theologian. In 1599, in a weather sermon delivered in the city of Tübingen, Sigwart told the assembled that 'the Almighty has exercised his merciful will here'. The only solution to the climatic crisis, he said, was for 'every man [to] arrive at honest repentance', which might 'move our Heavenly Father to... make these punishments less severe'.

Weather sermons are back in fashion. Only they aren't a 'minor literary genre' anymore – they're the cash cow of publishing houses and film studios. Books with titles like *Angry Weather: Heatwaves, Floods, Storms and the New Science of Climate Change*, *The Last Generation: How Nature Will Take Her Revenge for Climate Change* and *The Uninhabitable Earth: Life After Warming* confirm that 'theological interpretations of climatic events' – as Blom describes the Little Ice Age's view of anomalous weather – are thriving once more.

And, again, the demand is made of us to 'repent' in order that we might make not God's punishments, but *nature's* punishments 'less severe'. In September 2021, Pope Francis and the Archbishop of Canterbury, Justin Welby, issued a joint statement saying humankind now has 'an opportunity to repent' for our failure to 'protect and preserve [nature]'.[39] A year later, Francis returned to the theme. Mankind must 'repent and modify our lifestyles' if we are to preserve 'our common home', he said.[40] It isn't only religious leaders who use this Little Ice Age language. Secularist greens do, too. One green writer once congratulated former climate-change sceptics in the media for having 'recanted' and accepted the truth of 'climate chaos'.[41] *Recant* – there it is, the fierce religious pressure of the past rehabilitated for a modern audience. To recant is to say one no longer holds an opinion or belief, especially one that is heretical. And there is little more heretical today than to question the climate-change narrative.

Climate change, the idea that humankind is having a negative impact on the planet, and what's more that there will be an extinction-level event if we do not radically change our behaviour, has become one of the most feverishly guarded orthodoxies of our age. You query it at your peril. It is one of the few beliefs for which an entire new grammar of censorship has been created to protect it from interrogation.

Describing, demonising and punishing 'climate-change denial' has become a veritable industry. There are books that search for the psychological origins of these apparently demonic thoughts. *Don't Even Think About It: Why Our Brains Are Wired to Ignore Climate Change*, one is titled. The author of that book, George Marshall, suggests that the 'in-group loyalties' that 'evolved' in the 'hunter-gatherer era' may be an 'obstacle when dealing with a universal shared threat' like climate change.[42] Slaves to the evolutionary process, we're unable to see climatic dangers clearly.

Psychiatrists analyse the 'powerful psychological component' to people's 'blindness to scientific reality'. Apparently, 'millions of people share the phenomenon of climate denial' and something must be done about it.[43] A report in the *Guardian* in 2014 said 'neuroscientists and psychologists' were finally 'beginning to understand just why people behave so irrationally [on climate change]'. It's because 'our brains are wired to respond to short-term problems, not long-term risk'.[44] And so our brains must be fixed. Priests of old who were concerned about the influence of heresy sought to save men's souls – today's eco-priests, horrified by the heresy of climate denialism, endeavour to mend our minds. Not through rational discussion, though – we've already established that human beings behave 'irrationally' on climate change – but rather through the manipulation of language and thought. As a report from British think-tank the IPPR put it, 'the task of climate-change agencies is not to persuade by rational argument but in effect to develop and nurture a new "common sense"'.[45]

Once again, we encounter the Orwellian instincts of the new elites, where they seek to change language as a means of reshaping thought. As one British professor has said of the climate discussion, 'many more words and phrases will be invented to adapt our languages to the increasingly chaotic changes in weather and climate'.[46] Such top-down word invention is already taking place, and at great pace. The *Oxford English Dictionary* has welcomed the increased 'urgency' of the words and phrases that are used to talk about the climate. 'The very real sense of urgency that is now upon us is reflected in our language', says an OED spokesperson. Even the dictionary is now deployed to the end of reshaping minds on how to think about climate change.

In fact, the phrase 'climate change' is on the way out now. The OED notes that between 2018 and 2020 the use of 'climate crisis' increased almost 20-fold in public discussion, while the use of 'climate emergency' increased 76-fold.[47] The Media and Climate Change Observatory at the University of Colorado at Boulder has noted the US media's adoption of 'more intense terms' to describe climatic events. 'Linguistic experts' cheer the media's embrace of the language of catastrophe because it helps to 'convey to the public an increasingly urgent [climate] threat'.[48] Scientists, the UN and even protesters have played a role in pressuring the media to adopt more apocalyptic lingo: in 2019, Extinction Rebellion protesters camped outside the offices of the *New York Times* to demand that it use the phrase 'climate emergency' rather than 'climate change'.[49] Speak the truth on Armageddon! 'Word choices by the press in this field matter', say linguistic experts, 'because they are influential on public opinion'.[50]

Shaping public opinion through the manipulation of language is a key and terrifying theme of our times. In this case, the aim seems to be to force us all into the apocalyptic mindset, to coerce us into the realm of doom by making us think less about 'climate change' and more about climate chaos, climate disaster, even climate apocalypse – a term the *New Yorker* has used.[51] Dissent becomes all but impossible when such fanatical language is made dominant. How can one call for calm in relation to something like 'climate chaos'? How can one say 'humanity can fix this' in relation to something like 'climate apocalypse'? An apocalypse is the complete and final destruction of the world. There's no discussing that. There's no 'other view' on that. In manipulating public discourse to make it better reflect their own ominous and millenarian sense of dread about the climate, the elites narrow what can be thought on this issue, and what alternative solutions might be proposed. The language dictates the thought, the thought in this case being that we're in the midst of the End of Days 'and it's our own damned fault'.

The chilling crusade to manipulate both our psychology and our language in relation to climate change, both our minds and our speech, confirms that the elites believe there is no need for any kind of debate here. This is a 'settled' issue, they say. 'Case closed', as one newspaper headline said about the science on climate change.[52] Joel Kotkin describes this as '"the debate is over" syndrome'.[53] On everything from climate change to gay marriage, we're constantly told issues are 'settled', says Kotkin. No questions, no discussion, no need for 'rational argument', in the words of the IPPR. We're done. It's over. Shut up. As Kotkin says of '"the debate is over" syndrome' in relation to climate change, the effect is that an issue of 'great import' is 'buried by the seemingly unscientific notion that everyone needs to follow orthodoxy on an issue that – like the nature of God in the Middle Ages – is considered "settled"'. Where the frightened people of the Little Ice Age were expected to obey God's diktats as expressed in the weather sermons of their local priest, now we're expected to obediently nod along to the settled scientific opinion of the weather sermonisers of our era.

Our leaders really do exploit terrible weather events to sermonise to the throng, to instruct us on what to think and how to behave. In October 2022, President Biden said Hurricane Ian in Florida had 'finally ended [the] discussion about whether or not there's climate change'.[54] The heavens have spoken! The contrary wind has issued its decree! Climate change is real and no further debate will be tolerated.

Kotkin is right to describe the orthodoxy of climate change as 'unscientific'. That's because there should be no orthodoxies in science. Nothing should ever really be 'settled' in science. This is one of the most disturbing things about the climate-change / chaos / apocalypse discussion – its transformation of science from a humanistic and open-ended endeavour to gain greater understanding of the natural world into a religious-style truth that no one may quiz or blaspheme against. This represents more than 'cancel culture', more than another cynical effort by the elites to circumscribe what may be said on a particular issue. It represents an overturning of the virtues of the Scientific Revolution itself, and of that central freedom of Enlightenment: the freedom to question authority.

Consider how 'The Science' is talked about in relation to climate change. 'Science has spoken', said then UN secretary-general Ban Ki-moon in November 2014, as if science were a secular version of the Word of God.[55] Eco-protesters march behind banners demanding that we 'Listen to the science'.[56] 'I don't want you to listen to me, I want you to listen to the scientists', said Greta Thunberg to the US Congress.[57] Scientists have become gods, their word infallible, their instructions to be slavishly followed.

Even the Royal Society, that great institution of Enlightenment, founded in 1660 to expand mankind's scientific knowledge of the world, now pushes the line that 'the science is settled'. A few years ago, it wrote to ExxonMobil demanding that it cut off funding to organisations that deny the truth of climate change. Acknowledge 'the evidence', it said, in hectoring tones.[58] Yet as a small group of climate scientists reminded the Royal Society in an open letter: 'The beauty of science is that no issue is ever "settled", that no question is beyond being more fully understood, that no conclusion is immune to further experimentation.' 'And yet for the first time in history', they said, 'the Royal Society is shamelessly using the media to say emphatically: "case closed" on all issues related to [a scientific matter]'.[59]

The old Royal Society, the Enlightenment-era Royal Society, understood the unsettled nature of scientific inquiry. Indeed, its motto was *Nullius in verba* – on the word of no one. That motto was intended as 'an expression of the determination of [Royal Society] fellows to withstand the domination of authority'.[60] The Scientific Revolution tasked itself with questioning the authority of tradition, with breaking free of ancient orthodoxies in the name of natural discovery. Shakespeare distilled this expansive new imagination in the words of Hamlet to Horatio: 'There are more things in heaven and Earth / than are dreamt of in your philosophy.' Now, too often, science, or at least certain branches of it, plays the opposite role. It has become the new source of authority, drawn upon by isolated political elites to add the appearance of weight to their policies, so that they might be called 'evidence-based'. The science of climate change in particular is treated, as Kotkin says, as an orthodoxy we're compelled 'to follow'. *Science has spoken.* Even the Royal Society now speaks less about approaching the world 'on the word of no one' and more about 'verify[ing] all statements by an appeal to facts determined by experiment' – a fittingly lifeless phrase for an era in which even science sometimes finds itself marshalled to the task of correcting thought, controlling behaviour and punishing heresy.[61]

One of the most curious things about climate-change science is that it is one of the very few sciences that is fiercely protected from criticism and falsification. It has become fashionable in Anglo-American society to call scientific claims into question. Since the 1960s, the intellectual classes have been pondering the 'social construction' of scientific truth. *The Social Construction of Reality*, by Peter L Berger and Thomas Luckmann, was published way back in 1966.[62] French philosopher Bruno Latour was fawned over on campuses across the West for his theories on 'the social construction of scientific facts'.[63] Feminist philosopher Judith Butler thinks even biological sex is a social construct. Meanwhile, the cry goes up to 'decolonise the science curriculum', to weave 'Indigenous knowledge' – an equally valid way of knowing, apparently – into scientific discussion.[64]

Everywhere science is picked apart, dismantled, relativised, often in a way that undermines the entire project of scientific inquiry and its important search for knowledge. But climate-change science is never socially deconstructed. It is sacralised, made utterly unimpeachable, put beyond the grubby questioning of both the layman and the expert. Despite the fact that it is clearly more socially constructed than most other sciences. Despite the fact that it clearly embodies the moral and political obsessions of the new elites. In particular, their lost faith in modernity and their urge to 'shrink the human footprint' – that is, rein in the era of industry. Every science is fashionably decried as the mere embodiment of man's social priorities, except the one that most clearly is that.

This is because, when it comes to climate change, we're not really talking about science. We're talking about scientism. We're talking about the use of science to fortify political agendas. We're talking about the way the technocratic elites now marshal expertise in their fearful moral favour. And we're talking about the treatment of science, this science at least, as a god for a godless age, whose decrees must be blindly obeyed. We are facing 'catastrophe' and 'only science can save us', as the *Guardian* once put it.[65] That isn't science – it's religion. Hence why it is heresy, tantamount to blasphemy, to think or utter any thought that might wound, even slightly, this mystical and misanthropic worldview that calls itself science.

An essential task of the heretic is to bristle at orthodoxy, to be suspicious of consensus. As John Stuart Mill reminds us, in times of tyranny 'the mere example of non-conformity, the mere refusal to bend the knee to custom, is itself a service. Precisely because the tyranny of opinion is such as to make eccentricity a reproach, it is desirable, in order to break through that tyranny, that people should be eccentric.'[66]

Let us be eccentric on climate change, then. Let us refuse to bend the knee to the custom and rituals and self-flagellation of this religion that self-identifies as a science. And let us say the most unsayable thing of all – that modernity has not in fact destroyed the planet but rather has rendered it a more knowable and liveable place. Knowledge has expanded, freedom has become a reality, life expectancy has increased, poverty levels have fallen and the threat posed by calamitous weather has been better contained as a result of our industrial exploitation of nature's bounty to the end of creating a more prosperous world.[67] Our footprint on the planet is a wonderful, civilising thing, not a stain to be erased. It might be blasphemy to say that now, but as George Bernard Shaw knew: 'All great truths begin as blasphemies.'

Back to the Little Ice Age. It wasn't all witch-hunts. It wasn't all weather sermons. It wasn't all terror in the face of climatic uncertainty. No, modern science and freedom were born then, too. Those long, icy centuries contributed to the fall of feudalism and to the 'emerging era of markets, exploration and intellectual freedom which constituted the beginning of the Enlightenment'.[68] Even music became more beautiful. Philipp Blom says it isn't a coincidence that the most admired violins in history, including those of Stradivarius, were created in the middle of the Little Ice Age. It's partly because trees take longer to mature in severely cold weather, leading to denser wood with 'better sound qualities and more intense resonance'.[69]

How typical of our downbeat times that we mimic the bad of the Little Ice Age – its witch-hunts, its dread of weather – while turning our backs on what was good about that most tumultuous of human eras: the rise of freedom of thought and the unleashing of scepticism towards orthodoxy, including the orthodoxy of the witch-hunt. Even in their dark and cold world, they felt their way towards freedom and truth. In our world of comparative comfort and plenty, we're feeling our way back to superstition and fear.

Witch-Finding

1 Agnes Sampson: Who was the famous East Lothian midwife, and how was she accused, and then murdered, for witchcraft in Scotland?, *Edinburgh News*, 8 March 2022

2 Witches by Weather: The Impact of Climate in Early Modern Witch Trials, *Retrospect*, Edinburgh University, October 2021

3 James VI and Witchcraft, Philippa Gregory, philippagregory.com, 11 September 2018

4 Witches by Weather: The Impact of Climate in Early Modern Witch Trials, *Retrospect*, Edinburgh University, October 2021

5 Scotland Considers Pardon for Thousands of Accused 'Witches', *Smithsonian Magazine*, 6 January 2022

6 How Climate Change Spurred Witch-Hunts In Medieval Europe Before The Age of Enlightenment, *History Collection*, 27 August 2018

7 How Climate Change Spurred Witch-Hunts In Medieval Europe Before The Age of Enlightenment, *History Collection*, 27 August 2018

8 *The Discoverie of Witchcraft*, Reginald Scot (1584)

9 *Daemonologie*, King James VI of Scotland / King James I of England (1597)

10 How the Little Ice Age Changed History, John Lanchester, *New Yorker*, 25 March 2019

11 How the Little Ice Age Changed History, John Lanchester, *New Yorker*, 25 March 2019

12 *Nature's Mutiny: How the Little Ice Age Transformed the West and Shaped the Present*, Philipp Blom, Pan Macmillan (2020)

13 *Nature's Mutiny: How the Little Ice Age Transformed the West and Shaped the Present*, Philipp Blom, Pan Macmillan (2020)

14 The Witch-hunt in Early Modern Finnmark, Rune Blix Hagen, *Acta Borealia*, Volume 16, Issue 1, 1999

15 *European Magic and Witchcraft*, Martha Rampton, University of Toronto Press (2018)

16 Climatic Change and Witch-hunting: the Impact of the Little Ice Age on Mentalities, Wolfgang Behringer, *Climatic Change*, Issue 43, 1999

17 A nation through its people's eyes, *Herald*, 26 September 2007

18 13 climate criminals who should be in jail, Tom Walker, *Red Pepper*, 23 February 2016

19 The internet is finally turning on celebrity 'climate criminals', *I-D*, 26 July 2022

20 Good intent can prevent climate change catastrophe, Claire Fauset, *Guardian*, 23 August 2006

21 Jail climate criminals, not peaceful protesters, *Socialist Alliance*, 7 July 2022

22 Deceitful Tongues: Is Climate Change Denial a Crime?, William C Tucker, *Ecology Law Quarterly*, Vol 39, No 3, 2012

23 Deceitful Tongues: Is Climate Change Denial a Crime?, William C Tucker, *Ecology Law Quarterly*, Volume 39, No 3, 2012

24 The Scold's Bridle, Jenny Paull, lancastercastle.com

25 Climate denial ads to air on US national television, MarkLynas.org, 19 May 2006

26 Betraying the Planet, Paul Krugman, *New York Times*, 29 June 2009

27 Is climate change denial a crime?, Bioethics Research Library, Kennedy Institute of Ethics, Georgetown University, November 2016

28 Climate change is really Apocalypse Now, Cyril Christo, *Hill*, 17 July 2021

29 IPCC report's verdict on climate crimes of humanity: guilty as hell, *Guardian*, 9 August 2021

30 IPCC report's verdict on climate crimes of humanity: guilty as hell, *Guardian*, 9 August 2021

31 *Daemonologie*, King James VI of Scotland / King James I of England (1597)

32 Australian bushfires are a warning to the world, Jo Dodds, *Guardian*, 2 January 2020

33 Southern Europe battles wildfires amid 'apocalypse of heat', *El Pais*, 19 July 2022

34 Hell is coming: week-long heatwave begins across Europe, *Guardian*, 24 June 2019

35 Climate change is really Apocalypse Now, Cyril Christo, *Hill*, 17 July 2021

36 The floods of neglect, Jeremy Leggett, *Guardian*, 27 June 2007

37 *Six Degrees: Our Future on a Hotter Planet*, Mark Lynas, Fourth Estate (2007)

38 *Nature's Mutiny: How the Little Ice Age Transformed the West and Shaped the Present*, Philipp Blom, Pan Macmillan (2020)

39 Church leaders call for repentance over climate crisis, *Tablet*, 7 September 2021

40 Pope Francis calls on Christians to 'repent and modify our lifestyles' to save the planet, *America: The Jesuit Review*, 1 September 2022

41 The threat is from those who accept climate change, not those who deny it, George Monbiot, *Guardian*, 21 September 2006

42 *Don't Even Think About It: Why Our Brains Are Wired to Ignore Climate Change*, George Marshall, Bloomsbury USA (2015)

43 Climate Change Denial, *Psychology Today*, 12 January 2019

44 Your brain on climate change: why the threat produces apathy, not action, *Guardian*, 10 November 2014

45 Warm Words, IPPR, August 2006

46 Climate change and language change, Brigitte Nerlich, UoN Blogs, Nottingham University, 1 July 2022

47 Exploring the language of climate change – a special Oxford English Dictionary update, Oxford University Press, 21 October 2021

48 The language of climate is evolving, from 'change' to 'catastrophe', *Fast Company*, 12 June 2021

49 Arrests at protest over *New York Times*' 'unacceptable' climate coverage, *Guardian*, 22 June 2019

50 The language of climate is evolving, from 'change' to 'catastrophe', *Fast Company*, 12 June 2021

51 What If We Stopped Pretending?, Jonathan Franzen, *New Yorker*, 8 September 2019

52 'Case closed': 99.9% of scientists agree climate emergency caused by humans, *Guardian*, 19 October 2021

53 The spread of 'Debate is Over' syndrome, *Orange County Register*, 22 April 2014

54 Hurricane Ian 'ends discussion' on climate crisis, Biden says on Florida visit, *Guardian*, 5 October 2022

55 IPCC: rapid carbon emission cuts vital to stop severe impact of climate change, *Guardian*, 2 November 2014

56 Is Deep Adaptation flawed science?, *Ecologist*, 15 July 2020

57 'Listen to the scientists': Greta Thunberg urges Congress to take action, *Guardian*, 19 September 2019

58 Royal Society tells Exxon: stop funding climate change denial, *Guardian*, 20 September 2006

59 Climate Scientists Rebuke Royal Society for 'Bullying' in Scientific Controversy, Moyers on America, PBS, September 2006

60 Take nobody's word for it, Nessa Carson, *Chemistry World*, 28 April 2021

61 *History of the Royal Society,* royalsociety.org

62 *The Social Construction of Reality*, Peter L Berger & Thomas Luckmann, Anchor Books (1966)

63 *Laboratory Life: The Construction of Scientific Facts*, Bruno Latour, Steve Woolgar, *Sage* (1979)

64 Weaving Indigenous knowledge into the scientific method, *Nature*, 11 January 2022

65 Only science can save us from climate catastrophe, *Guardian*, 20 January 2008

66 *On Liberty and the Subjection of Women*, John Stuart Mill, Penguin Classics (2006)

67 See *False Alarm: How Climate Change Panic Costs Us Trillions, Hurts the Poor, and Fails to Fix the Planet*, Bjorn Lomborg, Basic Books (2021)

68 How the Little Ice Age Changed History, John Lanchester, *New Yorker*, 25 March 2019

69 *Nature's Mutiny: How the Little Ice Age Transformed the West and Shaped the Present*, Philipp Blom, Pan Macmillan (2020)

3

COVID AS METAPHOR

They told us not to speak to our neighbours. That conversation is death. That friendliness kills. While it might be 'human nature' to 'engage in conversation with others, to be friendly, unfortunately this is not the time to do that', said Kerry Chant, the chief health officer of New South Wales. 'Don't start up a conversation', she instructed.[1] The sight of people chatting left experts horrified. 'I still see neighbours talking to each other every day. I'm worried for them', said a doctor in Malaysia during one of its lockdowns. 'If you see your neighbours when you're jogging by the side of the road, you don't stop and talk', he said.[2] Canadian officials were a tad more generous. 'Can you talk with your neighbour over the fence…? Yes you can, as long as you're maintaining the two-metre distance', said Vera Etches, one of Canada's medical officers of health.[3] Actually, even that might be risky, said one health journal. It reported that 'sometimes six feet of distance while speaking' may not be enough to keep the disease at bay.[4] 'Normal conversation' remains perilous, it said, beneath a stock photo of that most chilling of visions in the Covid era: two people chatting in a park.

Commentators were likewise sickened by the sight of people talking. We need to discuss 'the importance of not talking in this pandemic', said a writer for the *Atlantic* in August 2020.[5] 'Mask up and shut up', the headline said. One American expert in disease transmission said that 'if everybody stopped talking for a month or two, the pandemic would probably die off'.[6] Save a life – shut your mouth. We were advised to use 'non-verbal communication' if we ran into friends or acquaintances. Try 'facial expressions, body movements and eye messages', they said.[7] Anything but dreaded, diseased speech.

Masks were feverishly embraced by some as a means of warding off not only Covid particles, but toxic conversation, too. 'They offer you a valid excuse not to speak to the colleague you bump into 16 [Tube] stops from the office', said a writer for the *Independent*. Better still, they protect you from the pollution of strangers' thoughts and germs. They 'provide an extra layer of defence from the person an inch from your face on the Northern Line who hasn't cleaned their teeth'. Masks kiss goodbye to that mad era in which we 'breathed and snorted and coughed over each other, letting germs and bugs run riot'.[8] Hell is other people, heaven is life in a face mask.

If you must converse, use technology, they said. University teaching was done virtually. School education – that noblest of tasks of transmitting the knowledge of a society to its young –took place on Zoom. So poisonous was real-life speech thought to be, so deadly were the droplets that accompanied our words, that even teaching was seen as too risky an endeavour. Go for dates online, they said. *Glamour* magazine offered '21 virtual date ideas that won't drive you insane'.[9] Have sex online, too, some said. And people did. A survey of 6,654 Brits aged 18 to 59 found that 53 per cent had engaged in virtual sexual activity during the first lockdown in 2020.[10] Being friendly to neighbours was out, wanking online was in. Experts declared that virtual conversation, facilitated by machines, would be the 'new normal'. Our 'relationship with technology will deepen as larger segments of the population come to rely more on digital connections for work, education, healthcare… and essential social interactions', said the Pew Research Center in 2021.[11]

But be careful online, too, they warned. Beware the 'infodemic'. An infodemic is when there is 'too much information, including false or misleading information, in digital and physical environments during a disease outbreak', explained the World Health Organisation

(WHO).[12] Virtual speech might be free of the diseased spittle that flies from the gobs of your real-life neighbours and colleagues, but it can still make you sick – misinformation 'causes confusion and risk-taking behaviours that can harm health', the WHO declared.

Online interaction, despite being droplet-free, was continually depicted as potentially polluting, like a Petri dish of intellectual bacteria. Metaphors of disease abounded in the discussion about online life during Covid. There is a 'pandemic of misinformation' on the web, said British politicians.[13] There's 'another pandemic', said *Science* magazine at the very start of all this in March 2020: 'coronavirus misinformation.'[14] We must protect people both 'from physical disease and the "disease of misinformation"', experts said.[15] 'False information has plagued the Covid response' and it is 'spreading virally', said one professor of communication.[16] Plague, spread, viral – we get it: ideas can be a disease, too. The solution, the professor suggested, was for social-media companies to 'remove content' that might very well be legal, but which is also harmful in that it can sicken the gullible that fall for it. Lies are the disease, censorship the cure.

So, if we ventured outside and spoke with a neighbour, we might get sick. But if we went online and spoke to someone thousands of miles away, we might also get sick. If we acted on our troublesome 'human nature' and struck up a conversation with a passer-by, we might be infected by his or her diseased speech. But if we surfed the web and joined a chat about Covid, we might be infected by people's diseased ideas. Physical malaise awaited us outside, moral malaise awaited us online. Covid-19 was the virus without; misinformation, in the words of one observer, was 'the virus within'.[17] Speech kills, whether with its spit or its lies.

No wonder silence was the dream of authoritarians in the Covid era. 'Silence was the silver lining of an otherwise appalling pandemic', said one writer about Britain's first lockdown.[18] '[In] a world full of noise and chatter', how beautiful to be reminded of 'the power of silence', said a writer for the *Harvard Business Review* when society came to a standstill.[19] Churches fell silent as singing was banned. Scientists even carried out 'spittle tests' on the choir in Salisbury Cathedral to assess 'hymn safety'.[20] If they found that spittle was being 'sprayed across an unsafe distance, causing possible transmission of the virus', then they'd suggest 'services could be hummed instead'. Even hymns kill. Even conversing with God is lethal. Funerals were even more deathly affairs than usual, with singing 'strongly discouraged'.[21] Singing was barred at the Proms, too.[22] They even wanted restaurants to be noiseless. Diners should 'eat in silence to prevent coronavirus spreading', experts advised.[23] As for the 'virus within', all those moral toxins on the internet, you could always protect yourself from that dangerous white noise if you 'log off and go do something else', said one expert.[24] Stop surfing, stop talking, stop singing. Just be quiet. There's a 'behavioural tactic' that might finally halt the march of Covid, said the *Atlantic*: 'That tactic is silence.'[25]

From the start, Covid-19 was both a physical threat and a metaphor. Both a real disease and a symbol. Both a serious sickness and an allegory for what the elites view as the sicknesses of human society. In particular, the sickness of unrestrained social engagement, of unchecked speech, of human noise. That was the true 'other pandemic': words, ideas, *us*. The problem was not only the foreign bodies of this new SARS, but also 'human nature' itself, our instinct to be friendly, to interact, to talk about things, including Covid.[26] Disease is often 'encumbered by the trappings of metaphor', wrote Susan Sontag in her classic work *Illness as Metaphor*.[27] Nineteenth-century diseases were seen as manifestations of defective character. In the ancient world, disease was considered an 'instrument of divine wrath'. 'Punitive notions of disease have a long history', Sontag said. And so it was for Covid. This disease became a metaphor for the supposedly toxic nature of modern human society, for the alleged contaminations of social life itself. And thus social control, the more severe the better, was the remedy.

The speed with which Covid was turned into a parable of human toxicity was extraordinary. Some of the metaphors of Covid echoed metaphors of diseases from earlier eras. We witnessed a return of the idea of disease as an 'instrument of divine wrath', or rather, in our case, of nature's wrath. It wasn't only daft Prince Harry who thought Covid might be a case of Mother Nature punitively reprimanding mankind for our destructive actions. '[It's] almost as though Mother Nature has sent us to our rooms for bad behaviour, to really take a moment and think about what we've done', Harry said.[28] No, serious people also wondered out loud if Covid might be Gaia's wrath for human hubris. '[N]ature is sending us a message', said the director of the UN Environment Programme, Inger Andersen, in March 2020.[29] Thanks to humanity's thoughtless meddling in nature, there have been 'too many pressures at the same time on our natural systems and something has to give', she said.

Green-leaning observers lapped up Andersen's pre-modern view of Covid as wrath. 'Nature is sending us a message with the coronavirus pandemic and the ongoing climate crisis', reported the *Guardian*'s environment editor. We're placing 'too many pressures on the natural world, with damaging consequences', he said.[30] Covid is a 'stern warning from nature', said a green campaign group.[31] 'How Covid is like climate change', declared a headline in *Scientific American*. Apparently, it's most like climate change in that it contains 'lessons' for humanity, one of which is that we must 'find ways of powering the planet without relying on fossil fuels'.[32]

Some of an eco-persuasion seemed almost to relish the harsh lesson Covid was sent to teach us. This disease is 'nature's wake-up call to complacent civilisation', said George Monbiot.[33] Our 'bubble of false comfort and denial' is being burst, he giddily declaimed. He appeared to welcome Covid's violent reminder that we are not as far above nature as we like to think. In the midst of this sickness, 'we find ourselves naked and outraged, as the biology we appeared to have banished storms through our lives', he said. Andrew Norton, of the International Institute for Environment and Development, said the new plague had brutally brought us round to the realisation that we must 'make sacrifices and accept restraints for both the common good and personal wellbeing'. And perhaps this will prise open our eyes to the further sacrifices we'll need to make if we are to 'address the climate crisis', he said.[34] Sacrifices to appease nature's wrath? It's a baleful cry our ancestors will have been familiar with.

Covid was envisioned as a supreme natural force that exposed the fundamental smallness of mankind. This sickness has 'shattered our illusions of safety', said a philosopher at Oxford University. It has 'reminded us that despite all the progress made in science and technology, we remain vulnerable to catastrophes that can overturn our entire way of life', he said.[35] French philosopher Bruno Latour said 'the germs' had made short work of our industrial society – they have 'put an economic system on hold everywhere in the world'.[36] In *Salon*, American professor and author Michael T Klare described Covid as a 'world-shattering event' and arguably 'nature's way of resisting humanity's assault on her essential life systems'. It's time to consider, he said, that we 'now live on what might be thought of as an avenging planet'.[37]

As Sontag knew, the interpretations of disease reflect the concerns and crises of the eras in which they strike. So the Plague of Justinian in the sixth century was seen as divine punishment for the many sins of man, and for the worldly excesses of Justinian himself. In the 19th century, syphilis was turned by some into a metaphor for mass democracy, then emergent. It was used to 'evoke the desecrations of an egalitarian age', says Sontag.[38] Ours is an era of a great turn against modernity, of repulsion with industry, of an exhaustion of faith in the project of mastering nature to the economic and moral end of making a world that works for humankind. Ideological concepts like 'the human footprint' and 'resource depletion' speak to our view of human interference in nature as a reckless, dangerous thing. In recent years, this political objection to humankind's pursuit of natural resources and greater growth has morphed into an objection to humanity itself. The post-1960s critique of a certain kind of human society – industrial society – has turned into a critique of humanity's very presence on the planet.

Consider the hyper-moralised terms that are frequently used to describe mankind. Humans 'are a plague on the Earth', says none other than David Attenborough.[39] The father of modern environmentalism, James Lovelock, once said 'the human species is now so numerous as to constitute a serious planetary malady'.[40] That view has trickled down into mainstream green thought, in particular the branch of it that frets over 'overpopulation'. Long before the emergence of Covid-19 there were open discussions about a contagious disease potentially acting as a corrective to the disease of mankind. Even organs as esteemed, and ostensibly rational, as *New Scientist* were wondering if a 'killer plague' might come along and 'save the planet' from people. 'It's getting overcrowded here on Earth. More than seven billion people are taking their toll on the planet and the number is rising', said a *New Scientist* piece in 2014: 'What would it take to defuse this population timebomb?'[41]

It was inevitable that in such a time, in this epoch of self-loathing, a pandemic like Covid would be conceived of as nature's rage against humanity, or at least as proof of the dangers of the modernity we have made. As one professor of human ecology said, that Covid was 'frequently imagined as nature's revenge on humankind' speaks to a now widespread belief that we are living through 'an epic tragedy in which the technological hubris of a Promethean [humankind] has destabilised and provoked a now avenging Earth'.[42] What we are witnessing is the secularisation of the idea of divine wrath. Now, plagues are not God's doing, but Mother Nature's; and it is less our sins and blasphemies that are being reprimanded than our pollution. 'Disease metaphors are used to judge society', said Sontag. And our society has been judged very guilty indeed by Covid – guilty of the hubris of imagining ourselves the commanders of nature.

Alongside Covid as a judgement on man's economic development, we had Covid as a judgement on our political development, too. This plague was viewed not only as a disease of globalised industry, but also as a disease of democracy. In this, it echoed the metaphors of syphilis. That STI was seen 'not only as a horrible disease, but a demeaning, vulgar one', says Sontag. Baudelaire thought little of speaking of syphilis in the same breath as democracy. 'We all have the republican spirit in our veins, like syphilis in our bones – we are democratised and veneralised', he said.[43] 'Syphilis was naturally a favourite metaphor for anything regarded as undesirable', writes cultural theorist Michael Kane, and was especially treated as a metaphor for 'democracy [by] anti-democrats'.[44] Covid went through a similar metaphorisation. For many intellectuals, this was a disease worsened by the excesses of democracy, and in particular by that political phenomenon they fear most – populism.

Populism is the dread of the elites. In the era of Brexit, Trump and other people-led pushbacks against establishment politics, the *ancien régime* of globalists and technocrats has come to see populism as the great scourge of our time. And lo, the pandemic, in their minds, was a sick and deathly expression of that scourge. Even before the emergence of Covid-19, some in the thought-leader set had talked about populism as a 'disease'. In 2017, John Keane, a professor of politics at the University of Sydney, wrote about the 'pathologies of populism'.[45] Populism is a 'disease of democracy', he said. It's a 'perverted response that inflames and damages the cells, tissues and organs of democratic institutions'. Gianni Pittella, a former first vice-president of the European Parliament, spoke of the 'virus of populism' in 2016, the year of Brexit and Trump. This virus is a menace to 'democracy, peace and stability', he said.[46] The pandemic intensified this intolerant view of populism as a foreign body in the bloodstream of liberal democracy.

The *Guardian* editorialised on 'pandemic populism'.[47] *Populists and the Pandemic*, an academic book published in 2022, argued that the populist policies of 'scapegoating, polarisation and disdain for expertise' aggravated the disease by giving rise to 'institutional paralysis'.[48] 'Populism has proven lethal in this pandemic', said a writer for the Council on Foreign Relations. He argued that 'those of us who are horrified by the populist surge of the past decade' have tragically witnessed a 'confirmation of our worst fears' – namely, 'that it really does matter for the wellbeing of the public whether politicians care about their citizens, believe in science, and are constrained by checks and balances that can rein them in when they go off the rails'.[49] *Confirmation of our worst fears*. This wasn't only illness as metaphor – it was also illness as ventriloquism. Covid was fevered proof of populism's sins. Magically, every criticism the liberal elites made of populism BC (Before Covid) was proven true by Covid itself.

In reality, there was little clear correlation between populist governance and 'letting Covid rip'. As Brett Meyer of the Tony Blair Institute for Global Change argued in his analysis of populism's response to the pandemic, 'most populists took [Covid] seriously'. Far from demeaning the science and encouraging their citizens to go about their business as usual, many populist leaders, including in India and Hungary, implemented 'excessive emergency powers' and 'harsh / biased enforcement measures'.[50] Those nations still experienced high levels of Covid infection and death, yes, but so did non-populist nations. Belgium, for example, had, for a time, the world's highest Covid death rate.[51] In its insistence that populist-led nations fared worse than others because of their blasphemies against expertise, the Council on Foreign Relations cites the example of Modi-ruled India.[52] It seems not to have crossed the minds of the populism-fearing elites that India's widespread poverty, ceaseless waves of internal migration and inadequate infrastructure might have played a more important role in shaping its Covid experience than the fact that a Hindu nationalist is currently in charge.

What was most striking was the feverish hope of some in the managerial elites that Covid might help to correct, to *cure*, the malady of populism. Covid was anthropomorphised as the reprimander of populist delusions. It was considered to hold a moral lesson for politicians as much as it held a wrathful lesson for capitalism. Writing in the *Atlantic*, Kurt Campbell and Thomas Wright expressed their longing that this lethal contagion would expose 'the limits of populism'. Let us hope, they said, that it teaches the world the following: 'Expertise matters. Institutions matter. There is such a thing as the global community. An enlightened response, even if it's unpopular, matters.'[53] Here, Covid was marshalled to do the dirty work of technocrats who were losing at the ballot box. Establishment figures may have failed to see off populism in the realm of democratic contest, but perhaps their political bidding might now be done by *germs*. Just as the old priestly class hoped plagues would add deathly weight to their moral messaging – behaving as the 'language of God's displeasure', in Priscilla Wald's words – so secularist thinkers today pray a plague will underline their call for a return to political normalcy.[54]

'*Expertise matters.*' That line in the *Atlantic*'s plea to Covid to help it vanquish populism really stands out. This is where we can see the supposedly true and just wrath of Covid – its wrath for people's turn against experts; its expression of a borderline godly displeasure with the sin of 'anti-intellectualism'. Past outbreaks of disease were seen as retribution for a people's turn against God and his Word – this 21st-century virus was seen as being most punishing for those who have turned against Experts and their Advice. As one academic study claimed, 'citizens with higher levels of anti-intellectualism' tended to 'engage in less social distancing and mask usage'.[55] And thus were they more likely to suffer, their ailments virtually a punishment for their profanities against expertise. It was fervently hoped that Covid's horrors might assist with the restoration of the pre-populist rule of experts. 'The experts are back in fashion', said a writer for the *Guardian* at the start of the pandemic. The era of Covid might just spell the end of 'Brexit's triumph of prejudice and romance over facts and figures', he said.[56] Imperial College in London, which provided the government with experts in the modelling of pandemics, crowed in March 2020: 'With the arrival of a global pandemic, experts are back – and with a vengeance!'[57]

Vengeance. What a striking choice of word. It means punishment for some injury or wrong. Which is fitting given that many in the establishment really do see populism as injurious to reason and sense, and thus deserving of the severest of admonishments. And if it takes 'the arrival of a global pandemic' to issue that admonishment, so be it. Here's the thing: few would dispute that expertise has an incredibly important role to play in a time of pandemic. Medical and scientific expertise were essential to demystifying Covid-19 and to inventing medical interventions, most notably the vaccine, that dramatically weakened its toll on the human body. However, the elite's cheering of Covid's 'rehabilitation of the expert' was no mere celebration of scientific insight and its deployment against a virus.[58] No, it was an expression of a broader effort to re-establish the *political* authority of the new philosopher kings – experts – over the 'low-information' public.

This is clear from the fact that it wasn't only those who disputed the pathological reality of Covid – so-called Covid deniers – who were accused of the sin of anti-intellectualism. So were those who raised questions about the *social* response to Covid, in particular the policy of lockdown. They were 'lockdown deniers'. Their questioning of government policy was considered as grave an affront to the expert class as the cries of those who said Covid isn't real, that it's all a 'scamdemic'. In lumping together social critique of lockdown and irrational opposition to the physical reality of disease, the media elites sought to delegitimise dissent across the board, to present even the democratic querying of policy as 'anti-intellectualism'. The self-avowedly vengeful return of the expert was as much about reasserting the dogmas of the technocrat class as it was about engendering respect for the medical battle against Covid.

Dissenters on lockdown were demonised to an extraordinary degree. A writer for the *New Statesman* went so far as to imagine them as devils from hell. 'Like Dante's inferno, Covid denialism is structured in concentric circles', he said. In the first circle are the populist politicians who are 'influenced by denialism and lockdown scepticism'. In the circles further down are 'the ignorant', those who speak of such things as the 'collateral damage' of lockdown.[59] So even raising the perfectly legitimate point that the wholesale shutting down of democratic life, educational life, economic life and global trade was likely to have undesirable consequences for spiritual wellbeing and living standards came to be treated as some kind of bestial fraud, best suited to hell.

Lockdown critics were branded a threat to public safety. They represent a 'dangerous trend', said a *Guardian* editorial.[60] The Great Barrington Declaration, which called for 'focused protection' of the vulnerable in preference to society-wide lockdowns, was treated as a blasphemous tract likely to harm life and limb. It is 'dangerous, unscientific and "total nonsense"', said the *New York Times*.[61] The *British Medical Journal* referred to the declaration's authors as 'merchants of doubt', as if doubt is bad, as if doubt were not once seen as the starting point of free, critical thought.[62] 'If you would be a real seeker after truth, it is necessary that at least once in your life you doubt, as far as possible, all things', said Descartes. Now doubt is tantamount to a sin. The *BMJ* slammed those who would 'sow doubt' over lockdown and said we must work towards the 'inoculation' of the public against such reckless thought. In short, we must protect people from that other pandemic – the plague of disagreement, the plague of wrongthink. In sections of the political establishment there was an urge to diabolise the sowers of doubt. Dominic Cummings, chief adviser to then prime minister Boris Johnson, called for officialdom to be 'far more aggressive' with 'all of these people running around saying… lockdowns don't work and all this bullshit'.[63]

From the very start of the pandemic, speech itself was treated as a potential threat, as its own form of plague. Officialdom's handwringing over our striking up of friendly chats with neighbours may have been underpinned by a worry about the diseased particles that might move from one mouth to another. But its dread of what was being said virtually, in the particle-free world of cyber but nonetheless public discussion, expressed a deeper foreboding about unfettered, unchecked, *free* speech. That is a disease, too. That is likewise a virus requiring intervention. Hence, all the talk of a 'pandemic of misinformation'. The World Economic Forum referred to it as 'information pollution', where 'false content and polarising narratives' were 'distorting healthy public discourse and impeding the effective implementation of public-health initiatives'.[64]

Pollution – that's how the new elite views our emission of ideas it disapproves of. And it's not an original take. As Sontag says, visions of 'pollution' frequently accompanied plagues of old. 'The medieval experience of the plague was firmly tied to notions of moral pollution', she says. The sick were considered to be morally corrupted as well as physically afflicted, as were the adherents to the false idol of anti-intellectualism during the Covid pandemic. In her book, *Contagious: Cultures, Carriers and the Outbreak Narrative*, Priscilla Wald explores how the word 'contagion' in the plague-ridden Middle Ages referred not only to the spread of sickness, but also to 'the circulation of ideas and attitudes'. 'Folly and immorality were more often labelled contagious than were wisdom or virtue', she says. 'Heretical beliefs and practices' were most likely to be referred to as 'contagious', she writes. And so it is today. The establishment characterises its own view on the social policies that are required to tackle a virus like Covid as 'expertise' – any questioning of its view is presented as a form of moral 'pollution', a 'disease of misinformation', a pandemic of lies, a 'plaguing' against correct thought.[65] Heresy remains the true and lethal sickness in the eyes of the knowers who rule over us.

Fundamentally, Covid was a metaphor for the alleged dangers of human freedom. This illiberal prejudice that treats unbounded human interaction as toxic predates the arrival of Covid. For years now, human speech and human relations have been discussed in the *lingua franca* of disease. Relationships are toxic, masculinity is toxic, parents are toxic.[66] Ideas are viral, content is viral, lies are viral. We speak of social contagion, emotional contagion, mental contagion, financial contagion. From the 1990s onwards, says Peta Mitchell in her book *Contagious Metaphor*, the 'extra-medical [language] of contagion' has 'flourished in contemporary discourse'. It all speaks to an authoritarian reimagining of the citizen, where we are no longer seen as free, capable adults who should be at liberty to think and behave as we please so long as we do not harm anyone else, but rather as toxic creatures whose thought and behaviour must always be controlled in order to protect others from the contagion of our wicked beliefs and the pollution of our everyday behaviour. This truth cannot be stated strongly enough: human beings were viewed as contagious long before the arrival of Covid-19.

This is the crucial thing to remember about lockdown. It represented not merely a practical effort by governments to control the spread of a disease, but also the full and final implementation of the pre-Covid view of humanity as a toxin to be quarantined. Indeed, even the idea of quarantine as a guard against other people's moral pollution predates Covid. Ours is the era of the Safe Space, of seeking refuge from hurtful words and harmful people in zones zapped of intellectual and spiritual danger. In his 2007 book, *Shopping Our Way to Safety*, Andrew Szasz coined the term 'inverted quarantine' to describe the modern trend for removing oneself from perceived environmental and human threats. The hyper-atomisation of our age has nurtured a view of people as poisonous, of ideas as dangerous, and of speech as a virus. Lockdown was the political victory of this modern species of anti-humanism, and a despairing defeat for the belief held by many of us that strong individualism and a strong sense of social solidarity are always preferable, especially in times of crisis, to fear and social retreat.

Lockdown has copper-fastened the vision of the individual as a pestilent creature, a plague not only on the Earth, but on other people, too. And it managed to achieve that, in part, through the quarantining of alternative ways of thinking – in particular, the belief that a more humanistic, socially galvanising approach to Covid would have been better than the blanket, forced isolation we were all subjected to. That liberal outlook now takes its place alongside ideas in the Middle Ages that were likewise viewed as 'heretical beliefs' that would worsen plagues. Our role in this era of diminished citizenship is not to think for ourselves, far less to think heretically, but rather to dutifully imbibe the ideology and instruction of the avenging expert class.

But a good heretic never does that. He never receives directives without question. And he certainly never agrees to suspend his faculties of thought on the grounds that the right way to think and behave has already been decreed by others. John Milton, in *Areopagitica*, said censorship's greatest offence is its 'disexercising and blunting [of] our abilities'. Only by being free to think for ourselves do we become fully human, he said: 'Our faith and knowledge thrives by exercise, as well as our limbs.' To police and shrivel the sphere of public discussion is to frustrate the search for truth itself, Milton said, by 'hindring and cropping the discovery that might yet be further made both in religious and civill Wisdome'.[67]

Truth is not something to be bestowed on us from on high – it is something we endeavour to discover ourselves through free thought, free debate and the free exchange of ideas with our fellow human beings. Resisting and challenging the libel that says humanity is a toxic force is the first step towards restoring the liberty and confidence we will need if we are to navigate whatever nature throws at us.

Covid as Metaphor

1 Australian health officer tells citizens to not talk to each other…, *Blaze*, 20 July 2021

2 Don't Chat With Neighbours In Person To Avoid Covid-19: Expert, *Code Blue*, 20 July 2021

3 'Yes' you can chat with your neighbour at a distance during COVID-19 pandemic: Dr. Etches, CTV News, 15 April 2020

4 Simply Talking Can Transmit the Coronavirus to Others, *HealthLine*, 26 February 2021

5 Mask Up and Shut Up, Derek Thompson, *Atlantic*, 31 August 2020

6 Mask Up and Shut Up, Derek Thompson, *Atlantic*, 31 August 2020

7 Effect of Face Masks on Interpersonal Communication During the COVID-19 Pandemic, *Frontiers in Public Health*, 9 December 2020

8 Why I will continue to wear a mask long after the pandemic ends, Rupert Hawksley, *Independent*, 5 July 2021

9 21 Virtual Date Ideas That Won't Drive You Insane, *Glamour*, 29 January 2021

10 COVID-19: Virtual sexual activity increased during first lockdown but young people had less sex, survey finds, Sky News, 17 December 2021

11 Experts Say the 'New Normal' in 2025 Will Be Far More Tech-Driven, Presenting More Big Challenges, Pew Research Center, 18 February 2021

12 Infodemic, who.int

13 Democracy under threat from 'pandemic of misinformation' online, UK Parliament, June 2020

14 Researchers are tracking another pandemic, too – of coronavirus misinformation, *Science*, 24 March 2020

15 Beyond the bedside: Clinicians as guardians of public health, medicine and science, *American Journal of Emergency Medicine*, December 2020

16 COVID misinformation is a health risk – tech companies need to remove harmful content not tweak their algorithms, Andrew Chadwick, *Conversation*, 21 January 2022

17 The Virus Within: How Misinformation Made the Pandemic Worse, Kathleen Doheny, *WebMD*, January 2022

18 Am I the only one who fell back in love with silence during lockdown?, Sarah Barratt, *Country Living*, 12 July 2020

19 Don't Underestimate the Power of Silence, Vijay Eswaran, *Harvard Business Review*, 22 July 2021

20 Scientists to carry out spittle test on Salisbury Cathedral Choir to assess hymn safety, Classic FM, 29 June 2020

21 Funerals to ban over 70s, only allow immediate family and be planned over Skype, Church of England announces, *Daily Telegraph*, 18 March 2020

22 Rule, Britannia! will be played at Proms but not sung, BBC confirms, *Guardian*, 24 August 2020

23 Don't talk while eating in restaurants, study warns, *Daily Telegraph*, 5 December 2020

24 Keep calm and don't spread misinformation, Gillian Andrews, MIT Press, 9 July 2020

25 Mask Up and Shut Up, Derek Thompson, *Atlantic*, 31 August 2020

26 Australian health officer tells citizens to not talk to each other…, *Blaze*, 20 July 2021

27 *Illness as Metaphor*, Susan Sontag, Farrar, Straus & Giroux (1978)

28 Prince Harry: COVID-19 pandemic almost like 'Mother Nature sent us to our rooms', Sky News, 2 December 2020

29 Coronavirus: 'Nature is sending us a message', says UN environment chief, Damian Carrington, *Guardian*, 25 March 2020

30 Coronavirus: 'Nature is sending us a message', says UN environment chief, Damian Carrington, *Guardian*, 25 March 2020

31 COVID-19, A Stern Warning From Nature, *Amazon Frontlines*, May 2020

32 How COVID-19 Is Like Climate Change, *Scientific American*, 17 March 2020

33 Covid-19 is nature's wake-up call to complacent civilisation, George Monbiot, *Guardian*, 25 March 2020

34 Coronavirus and climate change are two crises that need humanity to unite, *Climate Home News*, 12 March 2020

35 Covid-19 has shown humanity how close we are to the edge, Toby Ord, *Guardian*, 23 March 2021

36 What protective measures can you think of so we don't go back to the pre-crisis production model?, Bruno Latour, bruno-latour.fr

37 Avenger planet: Is the COVID-19 pandemic Mother Nature's response to human transgression?, Michael T Klare, *Salon*, 6 April 2020

38 *Illness as Metaphor*, Susan Sontag, Farrar, Straus & Giroux (1978)

39 David Attenborough – Humans are plague on Earth, *Daily Telegraph*, 22 January 2013

40 *Healing Gaia: Practical Medicine for the Planet*, James Lovelock, Random House (1991)

41 A killer plague wouldn't save the planet from us, Fred Pearce, *New Scientist*, 29 October 2014

42 Beyond the Image of COVID-19 as Nature's Revenge, Alf Hornborg, *Sustainability*, 29 April 2021

43 *Illness as Metaphor*, Susan Sontag, Farrar, Straus & Giroux (1978)

44 *Modern Men: Mapping Masculinity in English and German Literature, 1880-1930*, Michael Kane, Continuum (1999)

45 The pathologies of populism, John Keane, *Conversation*, 29 September 2017

46 Donald Trump is a 'virus', Gianni Pittella, *Parliament Magazine*, 4 August 2016

47 The *Guardian* view on pandemic populism: leads to sloppy lawmaking, *Guardian*, 29 September 2020

48 *Populists and the Pandemic: How Populists Around the World Responded to COVID-19*, Nils Ringe and Lucio Renno (eds), Routledge (2022)

49 How Populism Has Proven Lethal in This Pandemic, Yascha Mounk, Council on Foreign Relations, 26 April 2021

50 Did countries with populist leaders suffer more from COVID?, Brett Meyer, LSE, 23 August 2021

51 Why Does Belgium Have the World's Highest COVID-19 Death Rate?, *Foreign Policy*, 26 November 2020

52 How Populism Has Proven Lethal in This Pandemic, Yascha Mounk, Council on Foreign Relations, 26 April 2021

53 The coronavirus is exposing the limits of populism, *Atlantic*, 4 March 2020

54 *Contagious: Cultures, Carriers, and the Outbreak Narrative*, Priscilla Wald, Duke University Press (2008)

55 Anti-intellectualism and the mass public's response to the COVID-19 pandemic, *Nature Human Behaviour*, 28 April 2021

56 The experts are back in fashion as Covid-19's reality bites, John Harris, *Guardian*, 15 March 2020

57 Coronavirus and the return of the expert, Nelson Phillips, Imperial College Business School, 25 March 2020

58 The return of the expert?, Professor Christina Boswell, University of Edinburgh, 22 April 2020

59 The Covid deniers have been humiliated but they are still dangerous, Paul Mason, *New Statesman*, 6 January 2021

60 The *Guardian* view on Tory lockdown sceptics: a dangerous trend, *Guardian*, 4 November 2020

61 A Viral Theory Cited by Health Officials Draws Fire From Scientists, *New York Times*, 19 October 2020

62 Covid-19 and the new merchants of doubt, *British Medical Journal*, 13 September 2021

63 *Spike: The Virus vs The People – the Inside Story*, Jeremy Farrar and Anjana Ahuja, Profile Books (2022)

64 Will the world clean up 'information pollution' in 2022?, World Economic Forum, 24 March 2022

65 The two pandemics – Covid and lies, *British Medical Journal*, 24 November 2020

66 *Toxic Parents; Overcoming Their Hurtful Legacy and Reclaiming Your Life*, Susan Forward, Bantam (2002)

67 *Areopagitica and Other Writings*, John Milton, Penguin Classics (2014)

4

ISLAMOCENSORSHIP

What are we going to do about the explosion of hijabophobia in Iran? Hijabophobia refers to 'the rejection of the hijab', according to *The Oxford Handbook of European Islam*.[1] It's a 'gendering discourse hidden within Islamophobia', says a professor of gender.[2] It's a form of 'hostility to the hijab', said a writer for the *Huffington Post* in 2017.[3] Well, there was plenty of that on the streets of Iran towards the end of 2022. There was an orgy of hijabophobia. Women ripping off their veils, mockingly affixing them to the end of sticks and waving them like flags, throwing them on to bonfires, and dancing as they did so. All while throngs of people, of both sexes, wildly cheered them on. I'd call that hostility to the hijab.

Hijabophobia was everywhere in Iran in 2022. It followed the death of Mahsa Amini, a 22-year-old woman from Saqqez in Iranian Kurdistan. The Guidance Patrol – Iran's morality police, chiefly tasked with ensuring that women are correctly veiled – arrested Ms Amini in Tehran on 13 September 2022. Her offence was failing to wear the veil according to government standards. Her brother was told she was being taken for a 'briefing class' in a police station – that is, a quickfire round of religious re-education to remind her of the importance of covering up. But two hours later she was taken to a hospital. She slipped into a coma and died on 16 September. Police say she died of natural causes. Her family suspect she died after being subjected to a violent roughing-up. Rage erupted across the land. For weeks, Iranian youths marched and clashed with cops and made clear their opposition to the

Islamist theocracy. In particular, to its imposition of the mandatory hijab law on all women.

Hijabophobia? It looked like it. Apparently one form that this 'gendered' Islamophobia takes is the blanket treatment of the hijab as a 'symbol of oppression… a symbol of discrimination'.[4] The Muslim Council of Britain has criticised media outlets that link hijab-wearing with being 'oppressed or subservient'.[5] Well, women in Iran certainly link the hijab with oppression. For them it is unquestionably a 'symbol of subjugation', as one Tehran-born female academic says.[6] The placards waved by Iran's revolters attested to their view of the hijab as an instrument of subservience. 'My Hair, My Choice', they said. 'Did you know that letting your hair blow in the wind is a crime in Iran?', asked one. Are these people phobic?

One is also forced to wonder what would happen to these women warriors against theocracy if they were ever to visit the West. The UK, for example. Might they be shouted down here, charged with the thoughtcrime of Islamophobia? That has certainly been the experience of one of their fellow countrywomen: Iranian exile and stinging critic of Islamist patriarchy, Maryam Namazie. Now based in Britain, Ms Namazie is frequently branded an Islamophobe. In 2015, she was prevented from speaking at Warwick University on the basis that her denunciations of the oppressions of Sharia law are 'highly inflammatory and could incite hatred'.[7] (The ban was later overturned.) A columnist for the once liberal *Guardian* defended the students who would 'rather not give a platform to [Namazie's] rhetoric'. 'Recognising the pressure British Muslims are under… could it be that some students felt welcoming a person who believes Islam is incompatible with modern life would be wrong?', he asked.[8] Strongly worded criticism of Islam might hurt people's feelings, apparently. So such blasphemy must be silenced. Shut down the uppity Iranian woman.

During a talk on the immorality of theocracy at Goldsmiths University in London a few months later, Namazie was barracked by members of the university's Islamic Society. As she described it, they were 'repeatedly banging the door, falling on the floor, heckling me, playing on their phones, shouting out, and creating a climate of intimidation in order to try and prevent me from speaking'.[9] The mob had been inflamed by the president of the Islamic Society, who issued a statement in the run-up to Namazie's talk in which he said she is 'renowned for being Islamophobic'. Would the same fate befall the women of Iran who took to the streets in 2022 if they decided to come to Britain and spread the anti-theocratic word? Might they be harassed if they visited a university campus, with young British-born Muslims taking the place of Iran's Revolutionary Guards as their tormentors? Might the *Guardian* urge their censorship on the basis that British Muslims don't need to hear any more criticism of their religion?

And what would be the response if one of them appeared on TV here to demand an end to enforced hijab-wearing in their homeland? In 2018, during an earlier uprising against Iran's mandatory hijab law, the BBC interviewed one of the protesters. 'When I wear a hijab, it's like I'm restricted, I'm oppressed. When I don't wear a hijab, it's like I'm free', she said.[10] It was yet more hijabophobia, apparently. In its 2018 report on media coverage of issues relating to Muslims and Islam, the Muslim Council of Britain slammed that BBC interview as an example of the Islamophobic bias that infects the British media. It was a 'typical example of an omission of due prominence', the MCB decreed. The BBC gave us 'the subjective opinion of one woman's experience of wearing the hijab without the counterbalancing view', moaned the MCB. And as a result it will have left viewers with that most Islamophobic of impressions – 'that the hijab is generally oppressive'.[11] We can't have that. We can't have people entertaining the hijabophobic view that the hijab is a problematic garment.

In Iran, the punishments for criticising Islam or the regime are severe. The Islamic Penal Code of the Islamic Republic of Iran covers crimes involving the 'insulting [of] sacred religious values'. Insulting Islam or 'any of the Great Prophets' is punishable by death or a prison sentence of up to five years. Insulting the ayatollah is punishable by between six months and two years in jail. Sometimes 74 lashes are substituted for jailtime. In the UK, the penalties for criticism of Islam are not remotely as severe. But there are penalties. Here you'll find yourself accused not of blasphemy, but of Islamophobia. Here you'll be subjected not to physical lashes, but to a tongue-lashing – 'phobic', 'racist', 'bigot', all of it. Here you won't be locked up, but you might be locked out – exiled from polite society and blacklisted from campuses for your profane thoughts. It is a very real prospect that the women being censored in Iran and denounced as blasphemers for fighting against the mandatory hijab law would also be censored in the UK and denounced as Islamophobes if they were to speak heatedly here about the crimes of theocracy.

Here's what is most striking: it is very difficult to speak positively about the 2022 uprising in Iran without committing at least one of the speechcrimes of Islamophobia. In 1997, the British think-tank the Runnymede Trust offered a definition of Islamophobia that remains widely referenced in UK public discussion. It outlined all the 'closed' and thus problematic views on Islam, all the 'phobic dread' that people sometimes feel and express towards that religion. The 'closed' ideas include the belief that Islam is 'inferior to the West' or that it is 'irrational' and 'sexist'. So is it Islamophobic to say that Iran's system of governance, which is very Islamic indeed, is 'inferior' to ours? And that its treatment of its female population, justified in the name of Islam, is 'sexist'? The better, more 'open' view to take on Islam, says Runnymede, is that it is 'different, but not deficient, and as equally worthy of respect'.[12] So the religious ideas that dominate in Iran are not really regressive – they're just an alternative but equally valid way of organising society.

As for Islamophobia's cousin, hijabophobia, one writer defines it as one of those 'Orientalist representations' that arrogantly depict

Muslim women as 'oppressed victims of misogynist societies'.[13] So can we not say that Iranian women are victims of oppression? Or that the system that oppresses them – the *Islamic* system – is 'misogynist'? Is that Orientalism? Islamophobia increasingly appears as a euphemism for moral relativism. We are cajoled, via the threat of being branded Islamophobic, and thus morally unfit for public life, to suppress any moral judgements we might have of Islam and Islamist governance. The mantra that Islam is 'different' but not 'deficient' is really a slippery insistence that we never question any aspect of it, that we never think about the moral and ideological faults which, like *all* religions, it must surely possess.

That it is hard to speak positively about the 2022 revolt in Iran without sounding officially Islamophobic is a testament to the insidiousness of modern censorship. Censorship exists to circumscribe certain ideas, to contract what can be thought on certain issues. And one of the ramifications of our societies' crusade against Islamophobia is that people's thought and speech on everything to do with Islam has become more wary, more edited, more trepidatious. No one wants to make an illicit utterance, to commit the blunder of blasphemy, to give voice to a thought that might fall foul of one of the stern definitions of Islamophobia. And what can we say on Iran, on its irrational, sexist, morally deficient oppression of women, that will not in some fashion, even if accidentally, violate this new moral code that forbids focusing on Islam's shortcomings?

This is doubtless one of the reasons there was such a muted response to the Iranian revolt in liberal and radical circles in the West. As Joanna Williams has said, where the killing of George Floyd by police in Minneapolis in 2020 gave rise to weeks of street protests in America, Europe and beyond, and to ceaseless expressions of social-media solidarity with African Americans, there was far less public anger over the Iranian security forces' killings of *hundreds* of people for the crime of demanding equality and freedom. 'An unarmed, innocent woman has died at the hands of police officers', wrote Williams of Mahsa Amini. 'Yet the silence from big business, Premier League footballers and Hollywood A-listers is deafening.'[14] No knee-taking, no blacked-out squares on Instagram, no muscular statements about 'justice' from big corporations. There was occasional commentary from celebrities, and fleeting bouts of virtual concern. But mostly the response was muffled, passing and swiftly superseded by other issues of the moment, like the environment and trans rights.

This is a clear case of the policing of language leading to unsure thought and the enfeeblement of public discussion. Young people in particular, having been counselled for years on the sins of Islamophobia, on the importance of never thinking or speaking ill of Islam, will have been wordless in the face of something like the great Iranian revolt of 2022. This is a generation brought up on Islamophobia Awareness Month, a British initiative that teaches that it is wrong to be disparaging towards 'expressions of Muslimness', including the veil.[15] On lessons in school devoted to 'tackling Islamophobia'.[16] On the idea that the hijab can be 'feminist and empowering',[17] to such an extent that the anti-Trump Women's March movement in the US used a woman in a hijab as one of its key symbols.[18] And on the belief that you *never* criticise the hijab. To do so is phobic, bigoted, a giveaway of how 'closed' you are, how lacking in moral suss. Remember when Ofsted, the government department that inspects schools in England, was branded 'institutionally racist' for making the perfectly legitimate recommendation that its inspectors should raise concerns if they see very young schoolgirls of four or five in the hijab?[19] (Most Islamic teaching only requires girls to wear a veil at the onset of puberty.) A new generation will have imbibed the social instruction that derision of Islam is a species of bigotry, and this will have left them bewildered, literally lacking words, in relation to the uprising for liberty in Iran.

'Islamophobia' is really a secularised form of blasphemy law. We're witnessing a restoration of the edict against sacrilegious thought, only now it's justified in the civil language of protecting minorities from offence rather than the religious language of protecting God from scurrilous utterances. The key thing about all the various definitions of Islamophobia is that they do not only condemn racist commentary about Muslims – something we can all agree has no place in our society. No, they also proscribe, or dream of proscribing, the making of moral judgements about *Islam*. This is the most Machiavellian aspect of Islamophobia – it comes dressed in the garb of anti-racism, cynically appealing to the public's abhorrence of racial hatred, yet its chief aim is to hush criticism of a religion.

This was clear right from the Runnymede Trust's influential definition of Islamophobia in 1997. Runnymede described Islamophobia as a form of racism, akin to anti-Semitism. But its accompanying report on this new racial hatred, *Islamophobia: A Challenge For Us All*, made clear that criticising Islam itself can also be prejudiced. 'The term Islamophobia refers to unfounded *hostility towards Islam*', the report said (my emphasis).[20] There it is. Runnymede hawked the idea that certain criticisms of Islam cross the line from legitimate commentary into racial prejudice. The problem, it said, is 'closed' views on Islam. 'Phobic dread of Islam is the recurring characteristic of closed views', it claimed. Yet these 'closed' views include thoughts on Islam that many people, including Muslims and especially former Muslims, would consider entirely legitimate.

One such 'closed' view is the belief that Islam is 'static and monolithic' and 'intolerant of internal pluralism'. It's racist to think of Islam as an intolerant religion? Another 'closed' view is the belief that some Muslims 'use their religion for strategic, political and military advantage'. The report singled out an article in the *Observer* that used the phrase 'Muslim fundamentalism' and which argued that Islam had been 'revived by the ayatollahs and their admirers as a device, indistinguishable from a weapon, for running a modern state'. That's a 'closed' view, said Runnymede, evidence of 'phobic dread', because it implies that Muslims have 'an instrumental or manipulative view of their religion'. Yet most people would view this as perfectly acceptable political commentary. By any moral measure, it is not racist to accuse Iran's ayatollahs of using religion to fortify their rule.

The Runnymede report went further still, reprimanding the use of certain words when talking about Islam. 'Fundamentalism', for example. 'It is not, we believe, a helpful term.' One of its examples of wrongthink on fundamentalism was a 1981 newspaper article by novelist Anthony Burgess, in which he referred to the 'dangerous fundamentalism' of Iran's new rulers – the ayatollahs. So even calling the Iranian regime fundamentalist is problematic. That's how morally autocratic the idea of Islamophobia was from the very start. Runnymede even warned against misuse of the word 'Islamic'. You should avoid speaking of Islamic violence or Islamic fundamentalism, it said, because 'the use of the word "Islamic" to refer to terrorism or to oppression is deeply offensive to the vast majority of British Muslims'. Instead you should say 'Islamist', but be careful with that word, too – always remember, said Runnymede, that 'it is untrue to claim that all Islamists have a single political outlook'.

So don't say Islamic terrorism. Or Muslim fundamentalism. Don't say Islam is intolerant. Don't say ayatollahs use their religion for strategic gain. These are expressions of 'phobic dread'. This isn't anti-racism. It is a naked effort to circumscribe public commentary on Islam. It is the issuing of new commandments against blasphemous thought. Runnymede itself recognised that its highlighting of wrongthink on Islam might have censorious consequences. There's a danger that this approach 'stifles legitimate criticism of Islam, and that it demonises and stigmatises anyone who wishes to engage in such criticism', it admitted. And yet it forged ahead with its profanity-policing agenda, and 20 years later, in a follow-up report, congratulated itself for having increased 'awareness of Islamophobia'.[21]

The Runnymede view of Islamophobia trickled down through society. Community groups, universities, schools, police forces and the shapers of public opinion embraced the new idea that '*hostility towards Islam*' is a form of racism. Subsequent definitions of Islamophobia echoed Runnymede's. In 2018, the UK's All Party Parliamentary Group (APPG) on British Muslims defined Islamophobia as 'a type of racism that targets expressions of Muslimness or perceived Muslimness'.[22] As some commentators pointed out, the use of that curious word, 'Muslimness', rather than just 'Muslims', paved the way, once again, for the protection of Islam from questioning and reproval. 'The concept of Muslimness can effectively be transferred to Muslim practices and beliefs', critics said.

The APPG even called on the government to set 'appropriate limits to free speech' on issues relating to 'Muslimness' and proposed the setting of 'tests' to ascertain 'whether contentious speech is indeed reasonable criticism or Islamophobia masquerading as "legitimate criticism"'.[23] This was a cry for the establishment of a new Star Chamber, and a mind-reading one at that, one capable of determining which critics of Islam are acting in a 'legitimate' fashion and which are being 'racist'. It is proof of the authoritarian soul of the Islamophobia agenda that MPs were openly pleading with officialdom to decree which public utterances on Islam are righteous, and thus permissible, and which are false, and thus deserving of sanction.

The spread of these definitions of Islamophobia through society, into our political, cultural and educational institutions, has had a dire impact on freedom of speech and even social stability. Most notably, it has given rise to the extraordinary spectacle of people being publicly humiliated and reprimanded, *in the 21st century*, for the offence of demeaning Islam.

In 2016, British gymnast Louis Smith was suspended from his sport for two months after a video emerged in which he 'appeared to mock Islam'.[24] In the clip, filmed at a social event, an inebriated Smith can be seen pretending to pray and making a humorous aside about '60 virgins' (he meant 72 virgins, the number of women faithful male Muslims can expect to encounter in paradise). The tabloids branded it a 'shock video'.[25] Smith eventually recanted his comedic blasphemy, making a very public act of contrition. 'I recognise the severity of my mistake… I wholeheartedly apologise', he said.[26] Two months of being cast out from polite society into the social wilderness might be preferable to the 74 lashes blasphemers in Iran receive, but morally it's the same thing: punishment for offending Islam.

Smith's suspension and his solemn public repentance were not enough for some. They wanted him dead or mutilated. He was besieged by fanatics online. 'I am going to splash acid in your face', said one. 'We are going to cave your face in', said another. These fundamentalists – yes, Runnymede, *fundamentalists* – will have felt empowered by respectable society's penalisation of Smith. A society that punishes people for making fun of a religion cannot be surprised when adherents of that religion demand more, even harsher punishments. Suspension and acid – they live on the same spectrum of intolerance.

In 2019, the Asda store in Dewsbury, West Yorkshire, sacked one of its meeters and greeters, a 54-year-old grandad, after he posted a video of a Billy Connolly skit on his Facebook page in which Connolly makes fun of Islam (and other religions).[27] He was later reinstated. In 2020, a train conductor for West Midland Trains was sacked after he celebrated the post-lockdown reopening of pubs by writing on his Facebook page: 'Thank fuck our pubs open up today. We cannot let our way of life become like some sort of Muslim alcohol-free caliphate just to beat Covid-19.'[28] For that, for stating the truth that many Muslim nations are 'alcohol-free', he was robbed of his livelihood. In Iran, Muslim citizens are punished if they drink; in the UK, you're punished if you make fun of the fact that some Muslims don't drink. It took an employment tribunal, and the intervention of the Free Speech Union, for the train conductor to get his job back.

People are frequently No Platformed for wrongthink on Islam. There's Maryam Namazie. There's Nick Lowles, director of anti-racist campaign group Hope Not Hate, who was disinvited to an event organised by the National Union of Students on grounds of Islamophobia – that is, because he has 'dared [to] condemn Islamist extremism', in his words.[29] There's Richard Dawkins, who was barred from giving a speech at Trinity College Dublin over his views on Islam (he thinks Islam is 'the greatest force for evil in the world today'). Dawkins deserves public censure, said a writer for the *Independent*, because he refuses even to acknowledge the existence of Islamophobia. He thinks it is a 'non-word… a baseless, non-referential concept'.[30] Questioning the idea of Islamophobia is to modern Britain what questioning the truth of Allah is to modern Iran – a blasphemy, a punishable offence.

And there's Trevor Phillips, the former chairman of Britain's Equality and Human Rights Commission, who was suspended from the Labour Party over 'Islamophobia'. His speechcrimes included asking why more Muslims don't wear poppies for Remembrance Sunday and pointing out that a substantial minority of Muslims in the UK felt an element of sympathy for the 'motives' of the *Charlie Hebdo* killers.[31] That this was true – a 2015 poll found that 10 per cent of British Muslims aged 18 to 34 believed that 'organisations which publish images of the Prophet Muhammad deserve to be attacked' – made no difference.[32] Phillips had committed the sin of 'phobic dread', and truth was no defence. (Having endured his public shaming, he was later let back into Labour.)

Art and literature have likewise been sacrificed at the altar of never offending Islam. In the wake of the Danish Muhammad cartoons controversy in 2005, Richard Bean's play, *Up on Roof*, was tweaked ahead of its performance by the Hull Truck Theatre in Kingston upon Hull in order to remove its 'two or three references to Muhammad'.[33] The references to Jesus Christ remained, but the references to Muhammad were wiped. Because the theatre was 'utterly scared shitless', said Bean. The Royal Court Theatre in London cancelled the reading of a modern adaptation of Aristophanes'

Lysistrata because it was based in Muslim heaven and featured the virgins of paradise going on strike to try to discourage Islamic suicide bombers down on Earth.[34] A production of Marlowe's *Tamburlaine the Great* at the Barbican tweaked the scene in which Tamburlaine burns the Koran and also cut some 'disrespectful' references to Muhammad.[35] Even Marlowe must bow to the edicts of the 21st-century Islamophobia police.

More recently, cinemas in the UK pulled a film, *The Lady of Heaven*, following rowdy protests by groups of Muslims who damned it as 'blasphemous' for, among other things, depicting the face of Muhammad.[36] 'Allahu Akbar!', the crowd yelled when the manager of the Cineworld cinema in Sheffield told them the sacrilegious movie would no longer be shown.

The mob's successful slaying of *The Lady of Heaven* perfectly illustrated how the secular ideology of Islamophobia emboldens the regressive religious urge to crush blasphemous ideas and images. What was most striking about the protests against that film was the use of the modern language of offence and victimhood. 'We are very offended… We are very insulted and we have a right not to be insulted', said one leader of this crusade against blasphemous art.[37] There's a direct line from the Runnymede Trust's insistence that we should avoid using words that are 'deeply offensive' to Muslims and some Muslims' belief 25 years later that they have a right never to be offended. The ideology of Islamophobia licences intolerance. It invites people to make a performance of their offended feelings with the aim of having the thing that offended them expunged from public view. It has given rise to an Islamist veto over the cultural life of the nation.

Alongside culture, political discourse is shrivelled by the strictures against Islamophobia. Our ability to speak on social problems is frustrated by the demand that we be circumspect in our every comment on Islam. Consider terrorism. Or 'Islamic terrorism', as Runnymede warned us not to call it. Hundreds of people have been massacred by radical Islamists in Europe over the past decade. Scores in the UK alone, including 22 at Manchester Arena in 2017. And yet you run the risk of being thought Islamophobic if you tell the truth about the ideology that underpins these acts of apocalyptic barbarism.

Heeding Runnymede's suggestion that we separate the words 'Islamic' and 'terrorism', Britain's counter-terrorism police have openly considered ditching terms like 'Islamist terrorism' and 'jihadis' and replacing them with 'faith-claimed terrorism' and 'terrorists abusing religious motivations'.[38] The thinking, as one officer said, is that a change in language could help to bring about 'a change in culture'. Using words that have a 'direct link to Islam and jihad' does not 'help community relations', he said, so let's stop doing it. We're back to the realm of Orwellian re-engineering, of manipulating speech to control thought. The suggestion that certain words should be scrubbed from the dictionary of everyday speech is really about altering how the populace thinks. In this case, it's about stopping us from thinking about 'Islamic terrorism' and instead making us think of these violent acts almost as natural disasters, as nameless horrors, belonging to no one, expressing nothing. In Iran, they pass laws forbidding criticism of Islam; in the UK, the authorities fantasise about altering language itself so that criticism of Islam becomes impossible. The former outlaws certain thoughts, the latter dreams of making certain thoughts unthinkable in the first place by erasing the words that underpin them. 'Don't you see that the whole aim of Newspeak is to narrow the range of thought…?'

The police may not yet have officially separated the words 'Islamist' and 'terrorism', but the deconstruction of that allegedly phobic phrase is happening anyway. It is rare indeed to hear a figure of authority speak of 'Islamic terrorism' or even 'Islamist terrorism'. When then UKIP leader Paul Nuttall said the word 'Islamist' in relation to the suicide bombing of the Manchester Arena in 2017, he was roundly denounced.[39] The Muslim Council of Britain agitates for the further memory-holing of the word 'Islamic' in the public discussion of terrorism. It has criticised media outlets for using terms like 'Islamic gunmen' and for describing ISIS as an 'Islamic death cult'. It even rebuked the *Daily Mail* for giving too much prominence to a Yazidi woman's view that her enslavers in ISIS believed they were acting according to 'Islamic law'. It is wrong, says the MCB, to say 'Islamic' in relation to ISIS.[40] This is where the crusade against Islamophobia ends up – with the reprimanding of a newspaper for allowing a woman who was tyrannised and raped by Islamic fundamentalists to tell her story. Perhaps she suffers from 'closed' thinking on Islam? From 'phobic dread'?

The crusade against Islamophobia harms life and limb as well as thought and speech. Behold the 'grooming gangs' scandal, where police forces and local councils up and down England were often slack to act on the sexual assault and rape of hundreds of mostly white working-class girls by men of Pakistani heritage because they feared being thought of as racist or Islamophobic. Witness the case of the Batley Grammar schoolteacher in Yorkshire, who was hounded into hiding by a mob of Muslim fundamentalists – a phrase we're not even meant to use – for the crime of showing his pupils an image of Muhammad during a classroom discussion of blasphemy. Free speech has consequences, the cultural elite says. It hurts people's feelings, they say. The consequences of censorship are far more dire.

Censorship distorts reality. It discourages honest discussion about the problems afflicting our society. It incites us to lie to ourselves and to each other. It emboldens the regressive to seek harsher and harsher punishments for those who offend them. It obliterates culture. It prevents the performance of plays and the publication of books. It sanctions the persecution of those judged as speechcriminals. It leads to the turning of a blind eye even to rape. The crusade against Islamophobia, no doubt unwittingly, but no less forgivably for that, has birthed all of these horrors. It has given rise to a society that prefers the violent debasement of a working-class girl to the utterance of a phobic thought about a religion.

Censorship fosters the violence of entitlement. With its founding belief that some words and ideas are so wounding to people's psychic wellbeing that we have no choice but to silence them – or at least to slyly phase them out of public life – censorship incites intolerance. It abets hatred and brutality. For if words hurt, why should we not hurt those who utter certain words? If speech is violence, why should we not act violently towards those whose speech we hate? The trials of Salman Rushdie are proof of the unholy link between taking offence and taking vengeance. He lost the sight in one eye and the use of one hand for the crime of criticising Islam, for expressing what it is now fashionable to refer to as a 'phobic dread' of that religion. This is the price of Islamophobia, then: an eye, a hand. How astonishing that in an era in which one of the great novelists of our time was labouring under a death sentence for criticising Islam, Western civil society made it its mission to demonise criticism of Islam.

In the past, Rushdie was considered blasphemous. 'The most offensive, filthy and abusive book ever written by any hostile enemy of Islam', said one Islamist activist of *The Satanic Verses* when it was first published.[41] Now Rushdie would be accused of Islamophobia. In *Joseph Anton: A Memoir*, the story of his life in hiding, Rushdie described Islamophobia as 'an addition to the vocabulary of… Newspeak'. That Orwellian term is the enemy of 'analysis, reason and dispute', he said.[42]

It's time to face the fact that the fatwa won. The appalling ideology of that death warrant issued by Iran against Rushdie in 1989 has perversely been internalised by Western civil society. Iran knows this. In a written response to the UN Human Rights Office, it welcomed the international treatment of Islamophobia as a 'social / cultural malady' and called for more 'legislative measures' against it. The ayatollahs are laughing at us. They cannot believe we have imbibed their bigoted hostility to blasphemous speech. That we have willingly become outposts of their regime of Islamic censorship. That we discourage criticism of the hijab, just as they do. That we punish mockery of Islamic beliefs, just as they do. That we consider hostility to Islam to be a sickness – a 'phobia', a 'malady' – just as they do. No self-respecting heretic silences himself to avoid offending a religion or a god or a prophet or Iran or any other ideology or belief system.

In Rushdie's words: '"Respect for religion" has become a code phrase meaning "fear of religion". Religions, like all other ideas, deserve criticism, satire and, yes, our fearless disrespect.'

Fearless disrespect – that should be the fuel of the heresy we need today.

1 *The Oxford Handbook of European Islam*, Jocelyne Cesari (ed.), Oxford University Press (2014)

2 *Pedagogies of Deveiling: Muslim Girls and the Hijab Discourse*, Manal Hamzeh, Information Age Publishing, 2012

3 The European Court Has Normalised Hijabophobia, *Huffington Post*, 15 March 2017

4 *Framing Hijab in the European Mind*, Ghufran Khir-Allah, Springer (2021)

5 Muslim Council of Great Britain campaigns for 'fairer' media coverage, BBC News, 9 July 2019

6 Iranian women burning their hijabs are striking at the Islamic Republic's brand, *Conversation*, 5 October 2022

7 Student union blocks speech by 'inflammatory' anti-sharia activist, *Guardian*, 26 September 2015

8 There's nothing misguided about the left's concern for Muslims, David Shariatmadari, *Guardian*, 1 October 2015

9 Muslim students try to disrupt ex-Muslim Maryam Namazie's talk on blasphemy at Goldsmiths University, National Secular Society, 3 December 2015

10 When I don't wear the hijab, it's like I'm free, BBC 100 Women, 7 December 2018

11 *State of Media Reporting on Islam and Muslims*, Centre for Media Monitoring, Muslim Council of Britain, Oct-Dec 2018

12 *Islamophobia: A Challenge For us All*, Runnymede Trust (1997)

13 Marketing an imagined Muslim woman: *Muslim Girl* magazine and the politics of race, gender and representation, Shelina Kassam, *Social Identities: Journal for the Study of Race, Nation and Culture*, June 2011

14 Mahsa Amini and the bravery of Iran's anti-hijab protesters, Joanna Williams, *spiked*, 21 September 2022

15 Islamophobia Awareness Month: 10 Years, islamophobia-awareness.org

16 Tackling Islamophobia, Children's Commissioner for Wales, 2018

17 The hijab has liberated me from society's expectations of women, Nadiya Takolia, *Guardian*, 28 May 2012

18 The Women's March that Welcomed the Hijab as a sign of Dissidence: Pink, Rainbows, and an American-flag Hijab, *Interdisciplinary Perspectives on Equality and Diversity*, 2017

19 Ofsted accused of racism over hijab questioning in primary schools, *Guardian*, 28 November 2017

20 *Islamophobia: A Challenge For us All*, Runnymede Trust (1997)

21 Islamophobia: Still a Challenge For Us All, Runnymede Trust, 2017

22 Islamophobia Defined, All Party Parliamentary Group on British Muslims, 2018

23 Islamophobia Defined, All Party Parliamentary Group on British Muslims, 2018

24 Louis Smith lands British Gymnastics ban after video appearing to mock Islam, *Guardian*, 1 November 2016

25 Louis Smith apologises for shock video appearing to 'mock Islam' and joking about 60 virgins, *Mirror*, 11 October 2016

26 Louis Smith apologises for shock video appearing to 'mock Islam' and joking about 60 virgins, *Mirror*, 11 October 2016

27 Disabled grandfather is sacked by Asda after colleague complained about him sharing an 'anti-Islamic' Billy Connolly sketch on his Facebook page, *Daily Mail*, 24 June 2019

28 'Secular atheist' train conductor who celebrated pubs reopening by declaring he didn't want to live in an 'alcohol-free caliphate' wins unfair dismissal claim, *Daily Mail*, 26 November 2021

29 Anti-racism campaigner 'stopped from speaking at NUS event' over 'Islamophobia' claims, *Guardian*, 18 February 2016

30 If Richard Dawkins can't understand why he was no-platformed, then maybe he's not as smart as he thinks he is, *Independent*, 26 July 2017

31 Labour suspends race pioneer Trevor Phillips over Islamophobia, *The Times*, 9 March 2020

32 New poll shows significant minority of UK Muslims support attacks on *Charlie Hebdo*, National Secular Society, 25 February 2015

33 Censorship in the theatre, *Daily Telegraph*, 14 April 2010

34 I suppose I might get stabbed one day, Richard Bean, *Daily Telegraph*, 26 August 2014

35 Artists must always risk offending, Stephanie Merritt, *Observer*, 27 November 2005

36 UK cinema chain cancels screenings of 'blasphemous' film after protests, *Guardian*, 7 June 2022

37 5Pillars, Twitter, 4 June 2022

38 Police may drop 'Islamist' term when describing terror attacks, *The Times*, 20 July 2020

39 It's official: you're not allowed to say 'Islamist extremism', *spiked*, 2 June 2017

40 *British Media's Coverage of Muslims and Islam (2018–2020)*, Centre for Media Monitoring, Muslim Council of Britain, November 2021

41 *From Fatwa to Jihad: The Rushdie Affair and Its Legacy*, Kenan Malik, Atlantic Books (2017)

42 *Joseph Anton: A Memoir*, Salman Rushdie, Random House (2012)

5

RISE OF THE PIGS

The swinish multitude is back. Only we call them gammon now, not swine. A couple of centuries ago, at the dawn of the modern democratic era, the rabble that wanted more of a say in public life were looked upon as pigs. Today, they're looked upon as pig meat. I'm pretty sure that's a demotion. At least pigs are alive, and pretty intelligent, too. Gammon, in contrast, is inanimate flesh, unfeeling, unthinking, liable to decay. That's us, apparently. That's the throng now.

Gammon has become the insult *du jour* of the British left in recent years. They use it to refer to a certain kind of voter. Right-wing, pro-Brexit, angry, red about the face – hence 'gammon'. As one professor of politics put it, gammon is 'derogatory shorthand for older white male Brexit voters'.[1] These gammon-cheeked scourges of electoral politics, who are normally working class or lower middle class, are held responsible for all the supposed political ills of our time, especially populism. The 'meaty slur' of gammon, as the *Independent* describes it, is targeted at blokes who are drawn to 'right-wing or nationalist politics' and who bear 'more than a passing resemblance to a plate of boiled meat'.[2] These 'flushed, middle-aged Brexiteers' look like cuts of a 'hearty pork steak', says one observer,[3] and they're ruining the political life of the nation with all their 'ranting about Brexit and immigrants'.[4]

People with some knowledge of British history, and in particular of the historical struggle for democratic rights, might find all this talk of pig meat a little familiar. The metaphor of pigs has stalked the debate about democracy in Britain for hundreds of years. Indeed, one of the great democratic journals of the 1790s was actually called *Pig's Meat*. Why? Because it was a reply, week in, week out, to the anti-democratic prejudices of the establishment and in particular to Edmund Burke's handwringing over '*the swinish multitude*'. Burke viewed the revolutionary masses as the hoofish destroyers of culture, and radical pamphleteers responded with satirically piggish indignation. We demand 'The Rights of Swine', said *Pig's Meat* in 1794.[5]

Burke introduced the trope of the pig into political discussion in 1790 in his *Reflections on the Revolution in France*. A deeply conservative attack on the revolutionary tumult across the English Channel, *Reflections* fretted over what would follow if the nobility and the clergy were pushed aside by France's politicised hordes. 'Learning will be cast into the mire and trodden down under the hoofs of a swinish multitude', Burke warned.[6] There it was. The nightmarish vision of the swine, of the pig-like, unlearned crowd, overpowering what Burke described as 'the spirit of [the] gentleman, and the spirit of religion'. Radicals in England, stirred rather than horrified by what was happening in France, responded with great ferocity to Burke's piggy jibe.

Late 18th-century democratic agitators made themselves the spokesmen for swine. In 1793, there was the publication of an anonymous pamphlet titled *An Address to the Hon. Edmund Burke from the Swinish Multitude*. It giddily ran with the pig metaphor, contrasting the economic difficulties of the 'poor porkers' of England with the lives of luxury enjoyed by 'lordly swine' like Burke. It was hugely popular, sold under the counter in bookstores, pored over in taverns. Perhaps it's the ruling class who are the pigs, it posited – there you are 'gorging yourselves at troughs filled with the daintiest wash', it said, while we 'porkers are employed, from the rising to the setting sun, to obtain the means of subsistence'.[7] The pamphlet was later attributed to James Parkinson, a surgeon and political activist.

He put out another pamphlet, again anonymously, titled *Pearls Cast Before the Swine by Edmund Burke*.[8]

The swine kept on speaking back. *Pig's Meat, or Lessons for the Swinish Multitude*, a radical weekly, was published by Thomas Spence. Spence was a radical bookseller, hawking seditious pamphlets from his stall on Chancery Lane in London. He fancied himself the intellectual 'feeder' of 'pigs'.[9] He chastised Burke for 'very improperly term[ing] his starving fellow-creatures the Swinish Multitude'.[10] There was also *Hog's Wash*, published by Daniel Isaac Eaton between 1794 and 1795. Eaton was one of the great radical journalists of the late 1700s. He sympathised with the French Revolution, a risky position to take in England at the time. Between 1793 and 1812, he was prosecuted eight times for publishing politically seditious and blasphemous pamphlets. He revelled in giving voice to the swine. Thanks to the 'blessed fruits of the art of Printing… the scum of the earth, the swinish multitude, [are] talking of their rights!', he wrote in 1794.[11] Imagine pigs 'demanding that political liberty shall be the same to all – to the high and the low, the rich and the poor – what audacity!', said this self-styled hog.

This was the Age of Revolution, as Eric Hobsbawm described it.[12] The period from the mid-18th to the mid-19th centuries when there were revolutionary waves everywhere from the US to Haiti to France to Latin America. In England, though, revolutionary sentiment was heresy. The life of the radical was 'fraught with danger', in the words of Michael T Davis. Stigmatised as 'rabble rousers, subversives and members of the so-called unruly "swinish multitude"', radicals in England faced a 'barrage of conservative propaganda, official legal repression and government persecution', says Davis.[13] There was one group of people the radicals could rely on for support, however – their fellow swines in the multitude. In 1794, Daniel Isaac Eaton published a piece in *Hog's Wash* that said we should 'rid the world of tyrants'. It was interpreted by the authorities as an attack on King George III, and thus a seditious libel, and Eaton was hauled off to court once more. But the jury acquitted him, to wild public acclaim. People celebrated in the streets and even cast medallions in honour of this spokesman for swine, this agitator for the rights of the multitude.[14]

Alas, the law eventually caught up with the swinish rebels. As Geoffrey Bindman describes it, 'by the end of 1795, the government [of William Pitt] had got its act together'.[15] It passed two new laws against the heresy of radical agitation. First, the Seditious Meetings Act, which banned gatherings of revolutionary thinkers. And second, the Treasonable Practices Act, which banned the publication and distribution of any 'seditious' pamphlet. The laws were depressingly effective, essentially putting a stop to English radicalism, for a while anyway. Samuel Taylor Coleridge described the laws as 'detestable' and 'iniquitous', since their aim was to 'kill off all who promulgate truths necessary to the progression of human happiness'.[16] Radicals recognised the jig was up for the swinish multitude. One poetically wrote: 'Having destroyed the best men in the nation, / we SWINE if we are not mistaken / must screaming and gnawing our tongues for vexation; / be butcher'd and made into bacon.'[17]

Bacon – that's how the swine of England ended up during the Age of Revolution, fried and sizzled by the reactionary rulers of the day. Fast forward a couple of centuries and now they're gammon. Pig talk is back. Of course, today's fretters over democracy, and especially populist democracy, are too sophisticated, or at least too politically correct, to use phrases like 'the swinish multitude'. And yet, strikingly, they have been drawn back to swine-like language. They have reached, once again, for the metaphor of the hog. They are, in a repeat of history as farce, talking about the plebs as pig meat. From swine to gammon, bacon to a 'plate of boiled meat' – there's a grim linguistic consistency in the British elites' fear of the multitude.

Gammon, like Burke's swines, are viewed as the enemies of culture: unrefined, insensitive, lacking in due regard for the expert class. Use of this 'meaty slur' exploded after the vote for Brexit in

2016. According to one definition, it is a 'collective noun for white, middle-aged, furious-faced men who are heavily concentrated in the vast reaches of England's Brexit heartlands'.[18] So widespread was the use of the gammon slur in liberal and leftish chatter post-Brexit that, in 2018, the *Collins English Dictionary* chose it as one of its words of the year. 'Gammon: a person, typically middle-aged and white, with reactionary views, especially one who supports the withdrawal of Britain from the European Union', is the official dictionary definition of these piggy people.[19]

The monstrous vision of pig meat is central to the gammon insult. These pesky voters have a 'red meat complexion', one commentator said.[20] 'Meat' is the 'skin tone of almost every furious, spittle-mouthed wingnut ever to scream borderline racist nearly-questions at the panel on [BBC] *Question Time*', said the *Guardian*.[21] Pig meat became a byword for what the metropolitan elites view as those small-village Little Englanders who make deficient democratic choices. These people are 'ruddy-faced from countless pints of bitter in a village pub', said one observer. They 'espouse the benefits of leaving those banana-curve-measuring bureaucrats in Europe out on their arse', he said. And their physical appearance? It is 'ham-like... porky, even'. Why shouldn't these 'racists' be likened to a 'minging cut of overly salty pork best saved for dog's dinners'?[22] Feed the gammon to the dogs. That will fix our politics.

The 'porkers' of the late 18th century have been replaced by men with the look of a 'hearty pork steak' in the 21st century. And however much the deployers of the gammon jibe say it's only a reference to a person's complexion, so calm down, the fact is it echoes the old loathing of swine remarkably well. As one columnist succinctly put it: 'Gammon is pig.'[23] This slur 'reeks of class snobbery', she said, so it is 'no wonder it is popular with the socialist bourgeoisie who... talk about people as if they own them'. The writer who is said to have invented the insult of gammon – children's author Ben Davis – has likewise noted its growing use as a 'classist' barb.[24]

That's because gammon, like swinish multitude, is fundamentally a reference to people lower down the social ladder: culturally stunted, uneducated, too dim for politics. As Darren Howard argued in his study, 'Necessary Fictions: The "Swinish Multitude" and The Rights of Man', Burke's use of pig language to refer to the masses spoke to a view of the throng as 'less human than educated… men'; as lacking 'the fullest possession of a humanising trait, such as having a soul, rationality, a moral sense'.[25] Dehumanisation is central to the gammon panic, too. One left-wing writer describes encountering a 'nest of gammon' on social media – nest: are they pigs or insects? – and says these soulless creatures require 'regular spoon-feeding from the trashy tabloids' to tell them what to think.[26]

The thing that most tightly binds Burke's dystopian fear of the swinish multitude and the 21st-century dread of gammon is the question of democracy. It is not a coincidence that both of these pig-based slights emerged in moments of democratic upheaval. Burke viewed the French Revolution as the most extraordinary event that had ever occurred. 'All circumstances taken together, the French Revolution is the most astonishing that has hitherto happened in the world', he said.[27] He wasn't wrong. The French Revolution completely transformed the standing of the idea of democracy. As one historian has it, '[it] was only with the French Revolution that the word "democracy" changes from a term laden with negative implications to a term of praise'.[28] Brexit may have only been a ballot-box revolt rather than a full-on revolution, and it might not reshape our epoch quite as thoroughly as the French revolutionaries did theirs. But it was a historic democratic moment, and one which, yet again, reanimated the pigphobia of the establishment.

These nests of gammon, these creatures resembling slabs of meat fit mostly for dogs, are seen as unfit for political life. For Burke, the swinish multitude lacked the intellectual and spiritual depth for sensible political discussion. Cool-headed reformers 'can proceed with confidence, because we can proceed with intelligence', he wrote, whereas 'hot reformations' driven by men 'more zealous than considerate' always end horribly.[29] Burke feared the influence of demagogues, believing they would exploit people's insecurities for political gain.[30] These same fears attend the gammon panic. Gammon are viewed as lesser beings whose minds are the playthings of demagoguery. Hence, the image of their 'spoon-feeding from the trashy tabloids'.[31] Gammon are injudicious receptacles of hate and ignorance from on high. They '[spit] out talking points found in fascist organs like the *Daily Mail* – or, for those preferring something less intellectual, the *Daily Express*', says one definition.[32]

The gammon's greatest offence is their rejection of the learning of the expert classes. Where Burke worried that the reasoned life would be 'trodden down under the hoofs of a swinish multitude' in France, and possibly elsewhere in Europe, today's elites fear that gammon-coloured ignorance will trump the cool, correct thought of 'experts'. We are living through a 'howling democratic storm', says one observer, in which there are 'gammon-faced ragers against reason' who 'have had enough of experts'. The result is a 'society motored by ignorance, ideology and self-interest'. Well, let 'the attention-seeking clowns jig in the growing wind', he says, for 'there's a job to be done, and only grown-ups need apply'.[33] No gammon, no swine, no pigs.

It is striking that for all of today's discussion about so-called cancel culture, about whether it's acceptable or not to 'cancel' the speech of the offensive and the ignorant, one of the most terrible acts of cancel culture is rarely mentioned – the cancellation of democracy.

We are living through a furious carnival of reaction against the democratic ideal. The populist moment has dragged into public view the cultural elites' extant terror of entrusting political decision-making to the people. The votes for Brexit and Trump in 2016, and the victories of right-wing and non-woke parties everywhere from Hungary to Sweden to Italy, have given rise not only to establishment disappointment at voters for making 'the wrong choices', but also to a renewed hostility towards the very idea of democracy, towards the entire modern principle of permitting the multitude to choose its rulers and its nation's future direction. And underpinning it all is a deep distrust of ordinary people and their capacity for reason and sense; a belief that limiting free public discussion, or at least more tightly controlling it, is the only solution to the trials of our time.

The fallout from the British people's vote for Brexit and the American people's vote for Trump was extraordinary. Views that were once only expressed in the privacy of a boozy dinner party exploded into public life. People who once would only have dared to hint that the masses are pig-like in the comfort of their own homes, while clinking glasses with a likeminded highbrow, were now giving utterance to such corrupt thoughts in the public sphere.

We are no longer successfully keeping 'the mob from the gates', said Matthew Parris. We now know, he said, that 'huge numbers of voters' can be 'horribly if temporarily misled by false prospectuses, by lies, by unreasonable hopes and by sudden fears and hatreds'.[34] 'Ignoramuses should have no say on our EU membership', said the headline to a Richard Dawkins piece in the run-up to the referendum in June 2016. People just don't have the 'experience', said Dawkins, to pronounce on 'the highly complex economic and social issues facing our country'.[35] Philosopher AC Grayling bristled at the politics of the 'crowd'. '[Rule] by crowd acclamation is a very poor method of government', he said. We are 'foregoing thought', he insisted, and allowing the run of 'misinformation, distortion and false promises'. 'Tabloid urgings' should not set the political agenda, he said.[36] There it was: the view of the crowd as easily swayed by the demagogic antics of press barons and liars.

There were open cries to protect the rule of the knowledgeable from the emotionalism of the masses. 'Brexit teaches us the dangers of rule by referendum', said one former UN official. 'Letting policies with wide ramifications be settled by the emotions of the moment will only ensure that popular sentiment holds sway over informed decision-making', he said.[37] In an essay in the *Guardian*, madly titled 'Why elections are bad for democracy', Belgian writer David Van Reybrouck said of Brexit that 'never before has such a drastic decision been taken through so primitive a procedure – a one-round referendum based on a simple majority'. *Primitive* – a striking choice of word. The fate of a nation, of an entire continent, in fact, has been transformed by 'the single swing of such a blunt axe, wielded by disenchanted and poorly informed citizens', he said.[38] A pro-EU former adviser to the UK Conservative Party wrung his hands over the 'democratic extremism' of the Brexit era, for it 'takes a noble idea, that everyone's political views should count equally, too far'.[39]

What an interesting concept – democracy going too far. This was a recurring theme of the post-Brexit and post-Trump intellectual meltdown – that rule by the people is fine, but rule by dumb people, by the uninformed, by people who have been 'swayed by prejudice and emotion', is another thing entirely.[40] Hence, Matthew Parris distinguished between the crowd and the mob. 'I believed in the wisdom of crowds but not mobs', he said following the election of Trump in the US. Now 'the crowd and the mob have begun to merge into each other'. Today, courtesy of that most mass of mass media (the internet), 'ignorant hooligans can discover with a click on a keyboard that there are millions like them out there', and as a result democracy 'is being tested to its logical limit', said Parris.[41]

The distinction between the crowd and the mob echoed Burke's distinction between reform steered by educated elites and 'hot reformations' spearheaded by the ignorant. It also, of course, reflected the long-running historical tussle between representative democracy – in which public sentiment is filtered through institutions, is bound by checks and balances – and direct democracy, in which public sentiment bluntly rules. In the former, we're a crowd: the masses, still, but good. In the latter, we're a mob: the masses unleashed, the masses untethered from the tempering forces of checks and balances, and thus swayable this way and that by demagogic trickery and tabloid urgings.

As 18th-century French philosopher the Marquis de Condorcet said, one must distinguish between 'public opinion', which is shaped by the enlightened, and 'popular opinion… which remains that of the most stupid and the most misery-stricken part of the people'.[42] In more modern terms, democracy's old 'elitist sorting mechanism has slowly imploded', said Andrew Sullivan in May 2016. Where the institutions of representative democracy guard against 'the tyranny of the majority and the passions of the mob', more direct forms of democracy are now marshalling 'feeling, emotion and narcissism, rather than reason, empiricism and public-spiritedness', he said.[43] The people unleashed is the great terror of the elites.

Under the cover of attacking populism, the cultural and political classes are really attacking democracy. Democracy still enjoys, just about, enough formal respect for any open assault on it to be looked upon with suspicion. It would be a brave soul who stood up and said, 'Let's get rid of democracy'. So populism – the blunt axe of Brexit, the mob love for Trump – became a kind of stunt double for democracy. Populism was the punchbag of establishments frustrated with democracy itself, but incapable of saying so. Populism's sins – its granting of too much power to the uninformed; its treatment of the passionate view of the pleb as equal to the knowledgeable view of the professor; its cultivation of a public sphere in which information, including misinformation, enjoyed free rein – were really democracy's sins.

Occasionally, though, observers ditched the pretence that populism was their target and went straight for the jugular of democracy. 'Democracy is supposed to enact the will of the people. But what if the people have no clue what they're doing?', asked a piece by American political philosopher Jason Brennan, author of *Against Democracy*.[44] Trump won, he said, because 'voters are ignorant'. A few days after the vote for Brexit, a senior fellow at the Center on International Cooperation at New York University put it as plainly as it could be put in *Foreign Policy*. 'It's time for the elites to rise up against the ignorant masses', the headline declared.[45] The divide of our time, he said, is between the 'sane [and] the mindlessly angry', and right now the mindlessly angry are winning.

There it was in black and white, or red in tooth and claw, perhaps: the informed must wrest decision-making back from the dense; the 21st-century nobility must take back power from the swinish multitude. Such elitism wasn't just *talk*. Actions were taken which, had they been victorious, really would have represented a rising up of the elites against the masses. In the UK, the establishment agitated for the voiding of the vote for Brexit, of 17.4 million ballots, and the holding of a second referendum. In the US, Trump was depicted by the political and academic clerisy as an illegitimate president, installed in power by illegitimate means, and thus a false ruler. There were moments in the past seven years when it genuinely felt as though democracy might be overturned. We were continually on the cusp of the most appalling cancellation in this era of cancel culture: the cancellation of democracy, and by extension of freedom itself.

For here's the thing: every undermining of democracy is an undermining of the thing that makes democracy possible and *real* – freedom of speech. Anti-democratic sentiment represents one of the gravest erosions of free speech imaginable because it chips away at the foundational conviction of free speech – namely, that people, from the nobility to the multitude, from the elite to the gammon, have sufficient mastery of reason to be able to weigh up information and ideas and make moral judgements as to which ones are good and which ones are bad. In dislodging this faith in humankind, and presenting people as the easily swayable targets of nefarious actors, the new ragers against democracy harm not only democracy, but liberty, too.

Our era's dread of gammon, its fear of the rule of emotion over expertise, is rooted in a belief that people lack the moral and political depth to be able to withstand the deceptions of the powerful. Brexit is the handiwork of 'lobbyists and billionaires' who were 'wilfully manipulating the media and public opinion', said a Labour MP in 2017.[46] It is a tragedy for 'liberal democracy', said a writer for the *Observer*, that 'demagogic arguments are proving so resonant to so many'.[47] Nick Cohen pitied the 'gullible supporters' of 'demagogic nationalism'.[48] Indeed, the dim throng is even worse than the wicked demagogue who exploits them, said Cohen: 'Compulsive liars shouldn't frighten you. They can harm no one, if no one listens to them. Compulsive believers, on the other hand: they should terrify you. Believers are the liars' enablers. Their votes give the demagogue his power. Their trust turns the charlatan into the president. Their credulity ensures that the propaganda of the half-calculating and half-mad fanatics has the power to change the world.'[49] The end result of the colossal ignorance of the believers, of the ignoramuses, of *the people*, is a 'postmodern fascistic style', said Cohen: 'fascism with a wink in its eye and a bad-boy smirk on its face.'

Such demented alarm at the terrors unleashed upon the world by the suggestibility of the masses is not new. A view of the multitude as dangerously foolish has informed elitist contempt for democracy for as long as the idea of democracy has existed. Plato thought democracy had a tendency to undermine the expertise necessary to run a state. In England in the 1640s, Marchamont Nedham, an adviser to Oliver Cromwell, responded to the Leveller idea of expanded democracy by describing the masses as a 'rude multitude' that is 'so Brutish that they are ever in the extreames of kindnesse or Cruelty, being void of Reason and hurried on with an unbridled violence in all their Actions, trampling down all respect of things Sacred and Civill…'.[50] In short, too emotional. A hundred and fifty years later, as France shook, we had Burke's agitation with the swinish multitude. Fifty years after that, in the 1840s, one of the key arguments made by the elites against the Chartists' fight for the right of working-class men to vote was that those dregs were the most likely victims of demagoguery, 'more exposed than any other class in the community to be tainted by corruption, and converted to the vicious ends of faction'.[51] And 70 years after that, when women demanded suffrage, so-called experts insisted that 'woman is emotional, and... government by emotion quickly degenerates into injustice'.[52]

Now, despite our societies' payment of lip service to the idea of equality, we are still told that people are too moved by 'prejudice and emotion', too lethally believing, too exploitable by conmen to be able to make reasoned political decisions. The argument against democracy has been remarkably static down the ages, from the Ancient era to the revolutionary era to the woke era.

Today, in the epoch of mass society, the main vision is of the voter as frighteningly malleable, as being witlessly moulded by the modern machinery of advertising, memes, the ceaseless onslaught of virtual messaging and hot takes. Morris Ginsberg, a 20th-century British sociologist, argued that 'the political ignorance of the masses and their gullibility' was always being reinforced by 'the existence of highly developed machinery for steady and cumulative suggestion'.[53] This view of democratic man as victim of machine, twisted into unreason by forces more powerful than himself, has existed in one way or another for a long time, of course. The machinery doing the shaping might change over time, but the low view of the machine's target has been a constant. Marchamont Nedham thought it was fiery speeches that would bring out the throng's brutish side. In the late 1700s, it was the dreaded seditious pamphlet that was thought to corrode men's souls. As Daniel Isaac Eaton satirically put it, 'Before this diabolical Art [of printing] was introduced among men, there was social order'. There was no questioning of the 'unerring wisdom' of 'Princes and Priests'.[54] In the early 20th century, it was the newly emergent popular press that was said to manipulate thought and damage good sense, crushing 'beneath it everything that is different, everything that is excellent, individual, qualified and select', in the words of Spanish philosopher Jose Ortega y Gasset.[55]

Now, it's the villainous internet, and its neoliberal facilitators, that is viewed as the dictator of people's thoughts and votes. As

Carole Cadwalladr said in the *Observer* in 2017, 'a shadowy global operation involving big data, billionaire friends of Trump and the disparate forces of the Leave campaign influenced the result of the EU referendum…'.[56] We're putty in the hands of the wicked.

The fear of the machinery of manipulation – a public speech, a printed pamphlet, a propaganda campaign, internet 'misinformation' – really speaks to a fear of those being manipulated. Forget compulsive liars, fear compulsive believers, as Cohen put it. The elites' panic over the forces of demagogic control is entirely proportionate to their view of the people as susceptible to control. Right now, in the fires of populism, their fear of the mass media is nothing more than an extension of their fear of the masses. The untruths of the media concern them only inasmuch as they have a low opinion of ordinary people's ability to withstand untruth.

The argument of the anti-democrats, then and now, is that surely it would be better if society were governed by those in the know. By Plato's philosopher kings or Burke's 'spirit of the gentleman' or today's PhD-earning experts. Anyone but the swines, anyone but gammon, anyone but us. The answer has to be no. First, because that just isn't how democracy works. As David Runciman says, if you want 'the rule of the knowers', then argue for it. It's called epistocracy, not democracy. And it is 'directly opposed to democracy', says Runciman, 'because it argues that the right to participate in political decision-making depends on whether or not you know what you are doing'. 'The basic premise of democracy has always been that it doesn't matter how much you know', continues Runciman: 'you get a say because you have to live with the consequences of what you do.'[57] Those who want the rule of experts, the jurisdiction of the technocrat, should argue for it, and name it – it's not 'better democracy' or 'informed democracy', it's epistocracy, the direct opposite of democracy.

The second reason we should reject the rule of the knowers is the far more important one. It's because democracy is not a means to an end. It is not some mere mechanism for arriving at what someone has decreed – often wrongly – to be the best way of running society. No, the virtue of democracy lies in its mobilisation of the people to think and speak on issues of great importance. Democracy's wonder lies not in its outcomes – some of which are good, like Brexit, others of which are questionable, like that third term for Tony Blair – but rather in its exercise. Democracy invites us to find ways to make our voices heard, and to listen to other voices, and to judge the moral weight of all we hear. Democracy asks us to take ourselves seriously, and to take ideas seriously, and to enter the public sphere as citizens. Yes, the endpoint of a democratic process can often have a transformative effect on society – again, as with Brexit – but it is democracy's transformative effect on those who engage in it that is the principal thing. It demands that we take decisions, and take responsibility for those decisions. Sometimes we make good choices, sometimes we make bad ones – it's the act of *making the choice* that matters. It strengthens our moral muscles, makes real our role as citizens, and binds people together into a society of choosing. Democracy gives life and meaning to the freedom of the individual to think and decide for himself, and to the ties and connections that transform society from a place we merely inhabit into a world we shape and own and govern.

John Milton understood this. Milton trusted people to use their reason. When God gave Adam reason, he wrote, 'he gave him freedom to choose, for reason is but choosing'. Heresy is choosing, too. That's where the word comes from. 'Orthodox' comes from the Greek for 'right belief', heresy from the Greek for 'choice of belief'. That remains the dread of the anti-democratic elites – our choosing of our beliefs, and our choosing of our political path. It remains the task of the heretic to defend choosing, 'for reason is but choosing', in how he thinks, how he acts on the world, and what he wants the political destiny of his nation to be. Pigs, keep fighting for the rights of swine.

Rise of the Pigs

1 Left politics and popular culture in Britain: From left-wing populism to 'popular leftism', Jonathan Dean, *Political Studies Association*, November 2020

2 Gammon race row: why British Twitter is boiling over about a meaty slur, *Independent*, 17 May 2018

3 Gammon: Why is the term being used to insult Brexiteers and where does Charles Dickens come into it?, *Independent*, 15 May 2018

4 This is why the word 'gammon' is cooking up trouble in the UK, *Journal*, 15 May 2018

5 *The Political Thought of Thomas Spence: Beyond Poverty and Empire*, Matilde Cazzola, Routledge (2021)

6 *Reflections on the Revolution in France*, Edmund Burke, Oxford World's Classics (2009)

7 *An Address to the Hon. Edmund Burke; from the Swinish Multitude*, James Parkinson (1793)

8 *Pearls Cast Before the Swine by Edmund Burke*, James Parkinson (1793)

9 *The Political Thought of Thomas Spence: Beyond Poverty and Empire*, Matilde Cazzola, Routledge (2021)

10 *The Political Thought of Thomas Spence: Beyond Poverty and Empire*, Matilde Cazzola, Routledge (2021)

11 *The Pernicious Effects of the Art of Printing on Society, Exposed*, Daniel Isaac Eaton, (1794)

12 *The Age of Revolution: 1789–1848*, Eric Hobsbawm, Vintage (1996)

13 *Radicalism and Revolution in Britain, 1775–1848*, Michael T Davis, Palgrave Macmillan (1999)

14 A heroic journalist, Geoffrey Bindman, *New Law Journal*, 2 March 2012

15 A heroic journalist, Geoffrey Bindman, *New Law Journal*, 2 March 2012

16 A heroic journalist, Geoffrey Bindman, *New Law Journal*, 2 March 2012

17 A heroic journalist, Geoffrey Bindman, New Law Journal, 2 March 2012

18 UKIP have chosen an actual Gammon as London mayor candidate, *Metro*, 12 November 2020

19 'Gammon' is added to Collins Dictionary as word of the year, *Daily Telegraph*, 7 November 2018

20 Is it racist to call white men gammon?, *Huck*, 7 February 2018

21 Is it offensive to call ruddy-faced middle-aged Tories 'gammons'?, *Guardian*, 14 May 2018

22 Here's why everyone's kicking off about gammon, *NME*, 14 May 2018

23 Calling someone a 'gammon' is hate speech, Tanya Gold, *GQ*, 16 May 2018

24 I'm the one who coined the term gammon – and now I deeply regret it, Ben Davis, *Independent*, 15 May 2018

25 Necessary Fictions: The 'Swinish Multitude' and 'The Rights of Man', Darren Howard, *Studies in Romanticism*, Summer 2008

26 Is it racist to call white men gammon?, *Huck*, 7 February 2018

27 *Reflections on the Revolution in France*, Edmund Burke, Oxford World's Classics (2009)

28 *Athenian Democracy: Modern Mythmakers and Ancient Theorists*, Arlene Saxonhouse, University of Notre Dame Press (1996)

29 *Reflections on the Revolution in France*, Edmund Burke, Oxford World's Classics (2009)

30 Long may we laugh at our absurd demagogues, Toby Young, *Spectator*, 23 April 2016

31 Is it racist to call white men gammon?, *Huck*, 7 February 2018

32 Gammon, *Urban Dictionary*

33 The world is drowning in a wave of ignorance and self-interest, Chris Deerin, *Herald*, 29 August 2017

34 Can we trust the people? I'm no longer sure, Matthew Parris, *Spectator*, 12 November 2016

35 Ignoramuses should have no say on our EU membership–and that includes me, Richard Dawkins, *Prospect*, 9 June 2016

36 Professor AC Grayling's letter to all 650 MPs, *Skeptical Science*, 6 July 2016

37 Dangers of Rule by Emotions and Referendum, Shashi Tharoor, *Quint*, 24 June 2016

38 Why elections are bad for democracy, David Van Reybrouck, *Guardian*, 29 June 2016

39 Will too much democracy bring the United Kingdom to an end?, Garvan Walshe, *Conservative Home*, 30 June 2016

40 Will too much democracy bring the United Kingdom to an end?, Garvan Walshe, *Conservative Home*, 30 June 2016

41 Can we trust the people? I'm no longer sure, Matthew Parris, 12 November 2016

42 *Political Actors: Representative Bodies and Theatricality in the Age of the French Revolution*, Paul Friedland, Cornell University Press (2022)

43 Democracies end when they are too democratic, Andrew Sullivan, *New York*, 1 May 2016

44 Trump Won Because Voters Are Ignorant, Literally, Jason Brennan, *Foreign Policy*, 10 November 2016

45 It's Time for the Elites to Rise Up Against the Ignorant Masses, James Traub, *Foreign Policy,* 28 June 2016

46 What Brexit should have taught us about voter manipulation, Paul Flynn, *Guardian*, 17 April 2017

47 The shock lessons for liberals from Brexit and the Trumpquake, Andrew Rawnsley, *Observer*, 20 November 2016

48 Only true liberalism can thwart the demagogues, Nick Cohen, *Observer*, 24 September 2016

49 Trump's lies are not the problem. It's the millions who swallow them who really matter, Nick Cohen, *Observer*, 5 February 2017

50 In defence of the poorest hee, Brendan O'Neill, *spiked*, 29 November 2016

51 *Spirit of the Metropolitan Conservative Press*, Volume 1 (1840)

52 *Suffragette Sally*, Alison Lee (ed.), Broadview Press (2008)

53 *Democracy Under Siege: Don't Lock It Down!*, Frank Furedi, John Hunt Publishing (2021)

54 *The Pernicious Effects of the Art of Printing on Society, Exposed*, Daniel Isaac Eaton (1794)

55 *The Revolt of the Masses*, Jose Ortega y Gasset, WW Norton & Company (1994)

56 The great British Brexit robbery: how our democracy was hijacked, Carole Cadwalladr, *Observer*, 7 May 2017

57 Why replacing politicians with experts is a reckless idea, David Runciman, *Guardian*, 1 May 2018

6

WHITE SHAME

Do you remember white-shame summer? It was 2020. It followed the murder of George Floyd by a police officer in Minneapolis on 25 May. America erupted with riotous fury. There were protests around the world. And a key feature of it all was white self-loathing. It was as if a new species of religious hysteria had seized Western society. Whites got down on their knees, confessed to the sin of privilege, wept for the crimes of their ancestors. 'Repent, repent!', the cry went up. Literally. 'Lament, repent and apologise for biases or racist ideologies', suggested the Salvation Army to the fallen white folk of Christendom.[1] It was an orgy of self-flagellation. And it was one of the keenest testaments of modern times to what can happen when conformism supersedes reason.

Everywhere you looked in 2020 and its aftermath there were people repenting for their moral stain of whiteness. In Houston in June 2020, a group of whites literally kneeled before some black people and intoned: 'Father, we ask for forgiveness from our black brothers and sisters for years and years of racism!'[2] Official religious voices got involved, too. 'White Christians must seek atonement', said a Baptist news outlet.[3] Robert P Jones, author of the tellingly titled, *White Too Long: The Legacy of White Supremacy in American Christianity*, called upon 'white Christians' to 'start thinking about repair and repentance'.[4] Repent, repent!

Us 'white Christians' must 'repent of our prejudices', said none other than the Archbishop of Canterbury, Justin Welby. Welby made good on his cry for the scrubbing away of the transgressions of whiteness when he announced in 2021 that the Church of England would scour every church in the land for the merest hint of racism. All of the CofE's 12,500 parishes and 42 cathedrals were instructed to scrutinise buildings for any 'historical references to slavery and colonialism'. 'Some [statues and monuments] will have to come down', said Welby.[5] A racial exorcism, if you like, driving the devil of history's white crimes from the village churches of the present.

The godless among the whites repented, too. They may not have prayed or lamented, but they did kneel, they did bow. 'Taking the knee' was all the rage in 2020 and 2021. It started with American footballer Colin Kaepernick in 2016. He would kneel during the playing of the national anthem before games in protest against police brutality. But it really took off in 2020 and morphed with extraordinary speed from a symbol of black defiance into a gesture of white mortification. Everyone, from white millionaire CEOs of massive banks to white politicians like Keir Starmer, was genuflecting in the fashion of Black Lives Matter. Those who refused to kneel were damned as still suffering from the infections of white supremacy. When England fans booed England players for kneeling, one commentator condemned their 'shameful, hurtful' behaviour. Those 'racists, boneheads and people without compassion', he cried.[6] Kneel, and you're good. Fail to kneel, you're wicked. You're dangerous, too. The sacrilege of jeering this modern act of genuflection could have a 'profound impact on the wellbeing of black sportspeople', declared the *Lancet*.[7]

That the taking of the knee had become a supplicant display of white shame was clear from the fact that anyone who dared to describe it as such was instantly shut down. When then UK foreign secretary Dominic Raab said he would never take the knee because it is a 'symbol of subjugation and subordination', he was denounced for blasphemy. He's 'an embarrassment to our country', said one former MP. He must issue a 'fulsome apology', said the leader of the Liberal Democrats.[8] Recant your sinful, white words.

Some looked not to God but to psychology to explain the moral deformities in whiteness that would lead someone to reject something as simple as taking the knee. Pre-2020, during the Kaepernick controversy, *Scientific American* said 'high-power people' are often not very good at 'attending carefully to others' and are 'more likely to miss individual nuances in behaviour'. So it is not surprising that white sports fans – high-power people, apparently – 'misread the meaning of "taking the knee"'.[9] Not only must our souls be saved, but our minds, too.

One of the most chilling things in the cult of white self-abasement was the collectivisation of guilt for the killing of George Floyd. It wasn't only that white cop, Derek Chauvin, who was culpable for that dreadful crime – all whites were. 'White America, if you want to know who's responsible for racism, look in the mirror', said a writer for the *Chicago Tribune*. Apparently, whites directly benefit from atrocities such as Chauvin's killing of Floyd because it is these 'racist individuals and systems that keep you at the top of the hierarchy'.[10] A writer for *Time*, shortly after Floyd's death, described white supremacy as a kind of free-floating ailment – it 'moves in and through [your] lives, hearts, minds and spaces', she said.[11] Whiteness came to be viewed as a disease, a plague. A piece in the academic journal, *American Psychologist*, analysed the 'pandemic' of whiteness. The 'pathogens of the whiteness pandemic' are 'inexorably transmitted within families', it said. 'White parents [serve] as carriers to their children unless they take preventive measures rooted in anti-racism and equity-promotion', it continued.[12] Racism is airborne. You cough it and spread it and communicate it to your offspring. It is the plague of suburbia.

Soon, racism was being discussed in the same breath as Covid-19, as a disease that threatens to sicken the entirety of the Western world. Across the US during white-shame summer, local and state leaders were declaring racism a 'public-health crisis'.[13] In the *Lancet* in April 2021, Kehinde Andrews argued that the 'hierarchy of white supremacy creates an uneven distribution of resources', including in healthcare.[14] Racism is the white infection that ails black bodies. A headline in the *Guardian* summed up this new vision of racism as a plague-like curse: 'Racism isn't just unfair. It's making us ill.'[15]

Where the spiritual adherents to the religion of white shame called for repentance, the secular lot proposed a more psychological cleansing of the white malady. In workplaces and schools and universities, a vast apparatus of whiteness correction has been established. Campaign group Everyday Feminism offers 'Healing From Internalised Whiteness', a three-day training course to cure you of your 'internalised white supremacy'.[16] In the US, Whiteness At Work advises organisations on how to 'disrupt white dominant culture'.[17] 'Three ways employers can decentre whiteness in the workplace', offers one business journal.[18] Coca-Cola subjected its employees to workplace training which advised them, among other things, to 'be less white' – that is, 'less ignorant, less oppressive'.[19] White employees at AT&T were advised to confess their 'white privilege'.[20] Confess your sins in other words.

'Diversity training' has become a veritable industry. An estimated $8 billion is spent on such initiatives in workplaces in the US alone every year. The fad for racial re-education, for what really amounts to whiteness-correction therapy, has led to some truly bizarre enterprises. Consider Race to Dinner, where rich white liberal women in the US pay $2,500 for race experts to swing by for dinner and educate them about their 'subconscious' racism. 'If you did this in a conference room, they'd leave', says one of the Race to Dinner organisers. 'But wealthy white women have been taught never to leave the dinner table.'[21] This is where the secular creed of 'anti-racism' crashes into the more febrile religious vibe of the whiteness panic. It's like a Last Supper of self-loathing. Handing over thousands of dollars to racial re-educators smacks of the indulgences of the Middle Ages, when the wealthy would make financial payments to the Church or a charity to reduce the amount of punishment they had to undergo for their sins. Only now it's the transgression of whiteness rather than transgressions against the Word of God that people pay and plead to have absolved.

The fallout from the murder of Floyd was unlike anything the Western world had seen before. Its protests and rioting may have borne some resemblance to the race disturbances of old, but that's where the similarity ended. Where older uprisings, whether it was the Chicago Race Riot of 1919 or the Watts Rebellion of 1965, expressed black anger, the Floyd moment and its mad aftermath were primarily concerned with white guilt, white complicity, white shame. Where past revolts were expressions of frustration at the slow pace of *structural* change – in housing, the labour market, civil-rights legislation – the Floyd fallout concerned itself with *therapeutic* change, primarily with mending the diseased psychology of whites. And where historical street-fights had at their heart a belief in racial equality – the Watts disturbances, for example, were fuelled in large part by anger at segregation in housing – the post-Floyd era is one that reveres racial difference. The belief that a vast moral chasm now separates the races was summed up by a writer for *Time*, who feared that the outcome of the Floyd tragedy would be 'white silence and black pain, *perhaps forever*' (my emphasis). Why? Because of even 'good white people's blindness to how they are (unwitting) agents of white supremacy'.[22]

Such grim fatalism, such a fretful conviction that whites and blacks might always have competing interests, confirmed that this was not anti-racism as we once knew it. This was not an expression of that old noble, hopeful belief that a society could be created in which race did not matter, in which a person's character would count for more than his skin colour. No, the Floyd fallout represented the entrenchment and even the globalisation of something very different, of what we might even refer to as anti-racism's opposite – *identity politics*. This forever racialism, this religion that demands ceaseless white atonement for unending black pain, is one of the central planks of today's culture of intolerance. You question it at your own risk.

Racism in this new telling is not merely a poisonous ideology. It is not merely the failing of a society to create genuine equality for all, regardless of their heritage. No, it is an original sin. It is the West's tainted nature. It is the hereditary stain of white-majority societies, in particular the United States. In the tumult of the Floyd fury, a writer for *Slate* said that what we really need to talk about is slavery, for that is America's 'original sin'. Racism is 'the original, founding sin' of this nation, she continued.[23]

This echoed the view of American theologian and activist Jim Wallis, in his 2015 book, *America's Original Sin: Racism, White Privilege and the Bridge to a New America*. '[The] historical racism against America's Indigenous people and enslaved Africans was indeed a sin, and one upon which this country was founded', argued Wallis.[24] This parable of inherited evil, of sin being passed down from the first American whites to today's American whites, was frequently given voice in the madness of 2020. 'White people', said one writer, 'have inherited [the] house of white supremacy, built by their forebears and willed to them'.[25] Racism, then, is akin to a defective gene, one found in all whites, trickling through generations.

The intellectual classes have made great efforts to officially rebrand America as a nation founded in sin. The 1619 Project, a journalistic campaign spearheaded by Nikole Hannah-Jones and the *New York Times*, aims to 'reframe the country's history by placing the consequences of slavery and the contributions of black Americans at the very centre of the United States' national narrative'.[26] That is, it wants people to conceive of America as having been born in 1619, when enslaved Africans first arrived in colonial Virginia, rather than in 1776, when the Declaration of Independence was issued during the American Revolution. This is a reimagining of America as having emerged from evil rather than revolution, from crime rather than democracy. They want to mark America with its own sin, so that all might see it. Some people actually carried out such medieval markings during the riots of 2020. Witness the tearing down of a statue of George Washington in Portland in June 2020 and its daubing with that most fateful and sinful date: 1619.[27]

The re-envisioning of racism as a hereditary sickness speaks to the profound fatalism of the new elites. We are very far indeed from the fight for civil rights. Indeed, one of contemporary America's most celebrated writers on race – Ta-Nehisi Coates – expressly flips the worldview of Martin Luther King on its head. 'The arc of the moral universe is long, but it bends towards justice', said MLK. Coates sees it differently: 'My understanding of the universe was physical, and its moral arc bent toward chaos then concluded in a box.'[28] Coates seeks to dismantle the very idea of the American Dream. He writes of 'the Dreamers' – those who pursue the American Dream of work, happiness, family life and liberty. It is unlikely these people will ever wake up to the racial horrors of their nation, he says. '[You] cannot arrange your life around them and the small chance of the Dreamers coming into consciousness. Our moment is too brief. Our bodies are too precious.'[29]

Coates is often compared to James Baldwin, yet he utterly lacks Baldwin's moral optimism. Baldwin did not baulk from analysing America's racial injustices in his best-known work, *The Fire Next Time* (1963). But he retained a belief in a freer future. Blacks should try to 'make America what it must become', he wrote.[30] Coates, in contrast, sees change as impossible, or pointless, because racial division in the US is not a glitch or a failing – it's an indelible feature of the republic. 'In America', he writes, 'it is traditional to destroy the black body – *it is heritage*'. There it is again: the ideology of inherited evil, of a sin so great and so ingrained that it cannot be escaped, by anybody.

Coates' depressed view of America as irredeemable runs entirely counter to the visions of the civil-rights movement. As one of his critics argues, 'Coates emphasises over and over the apparent permanence of racial injustice in America, the foolishness of believing that one person can make a change, and the dangers of believing in the American Dream'.[31] Contrast that with Martin Luther King's shining, unshakeable faith in America and its promise of liberty. In the words of Elisabeth Lasch-Quinn, King 'appealed constantly to universal rights and dignity'. His emphasis on 'character' was not just because it is a more rational measure of a man than his skin colour, but also because character comes with 'connotations of self-discipline and obligation to the common good', Lasch-Quinn says.[32] A man's character is what made him fit for inclusion in the life of the American republic, King believed. He called on Americans 'to make real the promises of democracy'. Those promises are embodied, he said, 'in the magnificent words of the Constitution and the Declaration of Independence', which announced that 'all men, yes, black men as well as white men, would be guaranteed the unalienable rights of life, liberty and the pursuit of happiness'. In the March on Washington in 1963, King invoked the American people's 'sacred obligation… to rise up and live out the true meaning of its creed – we hold these truths to be self-evident, that all men are created equal'.[33]

This was the 'unrelentingly moral logic' of King's worldview, says Lasch-Quinn – that the key to black people's liberty lay in the universal values embodied in the very institutions and ideas of the American republic. The fatalism of what passes for 'anti-racism' today is a whole moral universe away from that outlook. Rather than drawing inspiration from the Declaration of Independence, today's race activists seek to dislodge it from its esteemed place in history and to make the arrival of slaves in 1619 the true birth date of America instead. Rather than fighting to make good on the founding belief of the American nation that all men have the right to life, liberty and the pursuit of happiness, the BLM generation damns America as a country born in the gravest moral error and likely to remain stained by it forever. As Coates says, racism in the US behaves almost like a 'force of nature', a mere expression of 'our world's physical laws'.[34]

And rather than struggling to supersede racial thinking, to finally replace judgements by colour with judgements by character, today's morally dejected activists see race as a forever prison. '*White silence and black pain, perhaps forever*.' They ossify racial thinking anew, categorising blacks as 'in pain' and whites as silent, complicit, psychologically deficient. Both the pathologisation of racism as a 'whiteness pandemic' and the mystification of it as an 'original sin' speak to a dread, dystopian conviction that racism is America's inoperable tumour, a permanent feature of the human experience.

What we are witnessing is not a second flourishing of the imagination of the civil-rights era, but the *subversion* of the civil-rights era. 'From civil rights to Black Lives Matter', headlines declared in 2020, with observers positioning the post-Floyd rage as the heir to the marches on Washington and Selma.[35] In truth, BLM and its politics of anti-democratic despondency represent a cultural revolution against the civil-rights era, a brutish coup against the universalism that King and others sought to make 'concrete, comprehensible and compelling'.[36] BLM is not challenging the grip of racial thinking on human society. It is restoring it, in the unforgiving language of political correctness.

Indeed, many in today's 'anti-racist' camp openly delegitimise King's best-known cry: 'I have a dream that my four little children will one day live in a nation where they will not be judged by the colour of their skin but by the content of their character.' Now, such moral colourblindness, such a desire to move beyond categories of race entirely, is itself cast as racist. A guide to 'Recognising Microaggressions', published by the University of California, Los Angeles (UCLA) a few years ago, rebranded 'colourblindness' as a racial microaggression. If you refuse to acknowledge people's experiences as a 'racial / cultural being', you are being problematic, it said. Its examples of colourblind microaggressions included: 'When I look at you, I don't see colour', 'There is only one race: the human race', and 'I don't believe in race'. Today it is the refusal to submit to the ideology of race, the refusal to view people as 'racial beings', that is the true racism.[37]

At the University of Wisconsin-Stevens Point, people who say they '[do] not want to acknowledge race' or who claim to be 'immune to races' are viewed as microaggressive.[38] A guide to 'inclusive terminology' at the University of Missouri recognised that the ideal of social colourblindness 'originated from civil-rights legislation', but it nonetheless decreed that such colourblindness is often 'disempowering for people whose racial identity is an important part of who they are'.[39] Numerous commentators now insist that seeking to overcome the racial gaze, the racial thought, is morally wrong. 'Colourblindness is counterproductive', said a headline in the *Atlantic*.[40] Heather McGhee, author of *The Sum of Us: What Racism Costs Everyone and How We Can Prosper Together*, says the problem with colourblindness is that 'a person who avoids the realities of racism doesn't build the crucial muscles for navigating cross-cultural tensions or recovering with grace from missteps'. Apparently, 'denial [of race] leaves people ill-prepared to function or thrive in a diverse society'.[41] So you should see race, you should approach the world racially. Forget character, think colour.

Gwendolyn RY Miller, a diversity consultant to educational institutions in the US, takes the cultural revolution against colourblindness to its dire logical conclusion. She lists even the following statement as a racial microaggression: 'Character, not colour, is what counts with me.'[42] Those are almost exactly the words spoken by Martin Luther King at the Lincoln Memorial 60 years ago. One is forced to wonder if MLK might be No Platformed today, cast out of academic and polite society for his stubborn preference for judgement by character rather than colour.

The new ossification of race has given rise to new forms of authoritarianism. To new cultures of censorship and even thought control. For if the races really are worlds apart – one morally diseased, the other threatened by that moral disease – then surely the only solution is to create a vast apparatus of race relations to try to maintain some semblance of social peace and linguistic decorum between these conflicting human tribes. That is what has happened. The race-relations industry has been growing since the 1950s. Frank Furedi, in *The Silent War: Imperialism and the Changing Perception of Race*, describes race relations as a 'defensive philosophy' adopted by the Anglo-American elites following the exposure of the barbarism of scientific racism during the Second World War.[43] In her 2001 book, *Race Experts: How Racial Etiquette, Sensitivity Training and New Age Therapy Hijacked the Civil Rights Revolution*, Lasch-Quinn traces post-King racial theories and activism, most of whose leaders tended to come out of academic culture and who were more concerned with 'emotional health' than structural change. In reimagining racial oppression 'in terms of incorrect attitudes or estranged emotions', these post-1960s radicals paved the way for the professional management of interracial interactions and speech that has exploded on campuses, in workplaces and across public life, says Lasch-Quinn.

White-shame summer, that strange act of therapeutic rage, is best seen not as a revolt against the elites, but as the militant wing of this elite thinking. As the physical enforcement of these ideologies of racial micro-management that have been gaining ground in the Anglo-American establishment for decades. As the violent furtherance of the political clerisy's loss of faith in the ideals of universalism and human dignity and their embrace instead of the misanthropic creeds of identitarian fatalism and racial control.

The central worry of the new racialists is whiteness. The moral panic about whiteness has almost completely pushed aside older moral panics about black deviance and black crime. Whiteness is now the dominant dread of our society's race-relations overlords. It is extraordinary how swiftly the word 'white' has come to mean problematic, or bad, maybe even evil. Consider the phrase 'too white'. You see it everywhere. Tom Perez, former chair of the Democratic National Committee, said New Hampshire was 'too white' to hold the first primary in presidential elections.[44] The *New Republic* casually described the US Department of Justice as 'too white'.[45] Here in the UK, a BBC chief admitted that *Monty Python's Flying Circus* probably wouldn't be made today because it was 'too white'.[46] We all know what 'too white' means – it means too privileged, too problematic, too toxic.

Indeed, the words 'toxic' and 'whiteness' are frequently put together in this era of white fear. The *Independent* reports on how one might 'heal from toxic whiteness'.[47] Political campaigners compile lists of 'toxic white progressives'.[48] Then there's 'toxic white masculinity', combining the sins of whiteness and maleness, apparently embodied best, or worst, by Donald Trump.[49] As we've seen, white detoxification programmes now abound in workplaces, all designed to re-educate whites out of their inherited prejudices and harmful behaviour. One of the most influential purveyors of the narrative of white toxicity is Robin DiAngelo, author and very well remunerated hawker of race training in workplaces. 'All white people', says DiAngelo, 'receive, absorb and are influenced by the racist messages continuously circulating across the society we live in'.[50] And any white person who claims he isn't is in denial. He is suffering from 'white fragility', says DiAngelo, which is when whites get defensive at the suggestion that the poison of white supremacy courses through their veins. That is, when they dare to question the judgement of such a high priestess of the new racialism as Ms DiAngelo when she decrees that they are members of a morally corrupt race.

As some observers have said, anti-whiteness rehabilitates the racist imagination every bit as much as a return of anti-blackness would. The fatalistic diagnosis of whites as sponges of racist messaging, programmed to absorb hateful signals from the culture that swirls around them, lands yet another devastating blow on the post-race vision of the civil-rights era. The likes of DiAngelo push 'a simple message', says Matt Taibbi – namely that there's 'no such thing as a universal human experience, and we are defined not by our individual personalities or moral choices, but only by our racial category'.[51] Again, the prison of colour wins out over the freedom of character.

Today's intensive re-racialisation of society doesn't only dent the dreams of the 1960s – it represents an intellectual assault on the Enlightenment, too. Indeed, much of today's anti-whiteness is really anti-Enlightenment, *anti-modernity*, in the drag of racial politics. Through their feverish rebranding of the intellectual and cultural achievements of the modern era as expressions of 'whiteness', the new racial ideologues dismantle, brick by brick, the gains of the enlightened era. Witness the assault on classical music for its 'whiteness'. The head of music theory at Juilliard, no less, recently decreed that 'it's high time the whiteness of music theory [was] examined, critiqued and remedied'.[52] Critics have slammed Beethoven's Fifth Symphony as a symbol of white male 'superiority and importance'. A writer for the *Washington Post* claims racism 'runs like rot through the structures of the classical-music world'. We are witnessing 'classical music's suicide pact', says Heather Mac Donald, as more and more institutions 'abandon the Western canon' to appease accusations of white supremacy.[53]

Or witness the panic over whiteness in the great museums of the West. The Museums Association in the UK frets over the 'invisible whiteness' of these institutions, where they apparently view all of human history through the white gaze.[54] Museums in the Anglosphere are urgently rethinking their displays to account for 'whiteness' overload.[55] The 'decolonise' movement, meanwhile, seeks to purge 'whiteness' from the teaching of literature and science. Undergraduates at Yale called on the English department to 'decolonise' its literature course and stop insisting that all students read Chaucer, Shakespeare and Milton. 'It is unacceptable that a Yale student considering studying English literature might read only white male authors', students said.[56]

Some universities in the UK have dropped Shakespeare and Chaucer to try to 'liberate their courses from "white, Western and

Eurocentric" knowledge'.[57] Science is reckoning with its 'whiteness', too. As one account says, 'recent years have seen an increasing number of calls to "decolonise science", even going so far as to advocate scrapping the practice and findings of modern science altogether'.[58] Apparently, modern science's obsession with evidence and truth is painfully white. It fails to incorporate the more organic intellectual approach favoured by 'Indigenous and other marginalised knowers'.[59]

Here, under the cover of a crusade against the sickness of whiteness, sections of the elite are giving vent to their moral exhaustion with modernity, their fatigue with Enlightenment and its burdens of truth and reason. Contemporary anti-whiteness speaks not only to the corrosion of the liberal elite's faith in the dream of post-race, but also to its turn against the bourgeois epoch itself.

Who loses out as a result of this frenzied countering of modernity that masquerades as a radical confrontation with whiteness? Everyone. Not just whites, but blacks, too. *Humanity.* In fact, if anything, elite anti-whiteness is more insulting to black people than it is to white people. The idea that black students are not really cut out for Shakespeare and Chaucer, or at least will have difficulty relating to such literary embodiments of historical whiteness, is plainly racist. It implicitly proposes the exclusion of blacks from the realm of great literature on the basis that its beauty and art is beyond their racial grasp, beyond their experiential understanding. The depiction of modern scientific thought as 'white', and museums' mission to expand humanity's knowledge of antiquity as 'white', and even Beethoven's Fifth Symphony as 'white', likewise has the baleful effect of locking non-whites out of these cultural kingdoms on the grounds that none of it is really their fit. It's too modern, too Western, too rational. And the idea that blacks are 'in pain', and that they require the performative penance of whites to validate and possibly alleviate that pain, turns them from citizens into patients; it makes them a special infantilised category of human being all over again, dependent for their therapeutic salvation on the coming to awareness of the truly central actors in modern society – white folk.

These are the wages of white shame. These are the consequences of the elites' racialisation of their own history and their own culture in order that they might more justifiably distance themselves, and us, from it all. We end up with the Enlightenment reimagined as racism, the discouragement of black learning, the further estrangement of the races from one another, and the cultivation of a new moral order in which we are instructed to view all whites as toxic and all blacks as vulnerable. A new moral order in which our thoughts are policed at work to cleanse them of internalised hate. In which our interactions in the public sphere are made evermore awkward by the demand that we think more of people's colour than their character. In which the very nations we inhabit are rechristened as sinful entities, pockmarked by the crimes of history, places we should feel estranged from, and maybe even ashamed of, rather than democratically connected to and morally invested in. Thus does the new ideology of race, and especially its cult of anti-whiteness, diminish citizenship, diminish equality and diminish culture.

Our lack of vigilance allowed this new anti-humanism to flourish. Failure to confront the politics of anti-whiteness, and to interrogate its intent, has rebirthed racism itself. Nothing better makes the case for full free thought and full free expression than the fact that, in their absence, in the subduing of those liberties by the new racialists who brand all dissent as bitter instances of 'white fragility', we have witnessed the undoing of the moral progress of the 1960s, and the diminishment of the cultural progress of the entire modern era.

The greatest heresy in the eyes of today's bleak gurus of racial correctness is the idea of *the human race*. Hence they demand that the statement 'There is only one race, the human race' be treated as a microaggression, a blasphemy against racial awareness.[60] Humanism, freely and unashamedly expressed, is their great dread, for it threatens their power over society and culture, which derives entirely from their cynical sorting of humankind into racial categories requiring either expert reprimand or expert therapy, depending on their skin colour. Universalism is their Kryptonite, the idea that poses the gravest challenge to their petrified racialism and their assumption of technocratic authority over the racialised masses. So let's give voice to the heresy of humanism. Let's reinvigorate King's constant appeal to universal rights and dignity.

We could do worse than to remind ourselves – and them – of the wonder culture holds for all of humankind, regardless of race. It was at the beginning of the 20th century, in *The Souls of Black Folk*, that WEB Du Bois baulked at the suggestion that 'negros' like him were not fit for 'the kingdom of culture'. He wrote: 'I sit with Shakespeare and he winces not. Across the colour line, I move arm in arm with Balzac and Dumas… From out the caves of evening that swing between the strong-limbed earth and the tracery of the stars, I summon Aristotle and Aurelius and what soul I will, and they come all graciously with no scorn or condescension… Is this the life you grudge us, O knightly America?'

1 Salvation Army defends guide telling white people to apologise for racism, *Denver Gazette*, 27 November 2021

2 White Christians Kneel, Repent, and Apologize to Black Believers for Racial Injustice, *Faithfully Magazine*, 8 June 2020

3 To heal racism, seek atonement before reconciliation, authors say, *Baptist News Global*, 17 March 2021

4 To heal racism, seek atonement before reconciliation, authors say, *Baptist News Global*, 17 March 2021

5 Church to consider removing or altering slavery monuments, *Guardian*, 9 May 2021

6 Pretending that booing England is about 'keeping politics out' is cowardly, *Guardian*, 6 June 2021

7 Taking the knee, mental health, and racism in sport, *Lancet*, October 2021

8 Dominic Raab criticised for comments on BLM protesters taking the knee, *Guardian*, 18 June 2020

9 The Psychology of Taking a Knee, *Psychology Today*, 29 September 2017

10 White America, if you want to know who's responsible for racism, look in the mirror, Dahleen Glanton, *Chicago Tribune*, 1 June 2020

11 Black and Brown People Have Been Protesting for Centuries. It's White People Who Are Responsible for What Happens Next, Savala Nolan, *Time*, 1 June 2020

12 The Whiteness pandemic behind the racism pandemic: Familial Whiteness socialisation in Minneapolis following #GeorgeFloyd's murder, *American Psychologist*, 2022

13 Racism is a Public Health Crisis, American Public Health Association

14 Racism is the public health crisis, *Lancet*, 10 April 2021

15 Racism isn't just unfair. It's making us ill, *Guardian*, 26 July 2020

16 Healing from Internalized Whiteness, Everyday Feminism

17 whitenessatwork.com

18 3 ways employers can decenter whiteness in the workplace and promote inclusivity, *Business Insider*, 29 November 2021

19 Coca-Cola faces backlash over seminar asking staff to 'be less white', *Independent*, 24 February 2021

20 'You are the problem': AT&T tells white staff they are racist, asks them to confess their 'white privilege' and to promote Defund the Police as part of re-education program by CEO John Stankey, *Daily Mail*, 29 October 2021

21 Why liberal white women pay a lot of money to learn over dinner how they're racist, *Guardian*, 3 February 2020

22 Black and Brown People Have Been Protesting for Centuries. It's White People Who Are Responsible for What Happens Next, Savala Nolan, *Time*, 1 June 2020

23 Why This Time Is Different, Dahlia Lithwick, *Slate*, 2 June 2020

24 *America's Original Sin: Racism, White Privilege, and the Bridge to a New America*, Jim Wallis, Baker Publishing Group (2015)

25 Black and Brown People Have Been Protesting for Centuries. It's White People Who Are Responsible for What Happens Next, Savala Nolan, *Time*, 1 June 2020

26 1619 Project, *New York Times Magazine*

27 George Washington Statue Toppled In Portland, Oregon Public Broadcasting, 19 June 2020

28 *Between the World and Me*, Ta-Nehisi Coates, Spiegel & Grau (2015)

29 *Between the World and Me*, Ta-Nehisi Coates, Spiegel & Grau (2015)

30 *The Fire Next Time*, James Baldwin, Dial Press (1963)

31 Ta-Nehisi Coates's 'Between the World and Me', *New York Times*, 17 August 2015

32 *Race Experts: How Racial Etiquette, Sensitivity Training, and New Age Therapy Hijacked the Civil Rights Revolution*, Elisabeth Lasch-Quinn, Rowman & Littlefield (2003)

33 *Race Experts: How Racial Etiquette, Sensitivity Training, and New Age Therapy Hijacked the Civil Rights Revolution*, Elisabeth Lasch-Quinn, Rowman & Littlefield (2003)

34 *Between the World and Me*, Ta-Nehisi Coates, Spiegel & Grau (2015)

35 From Civil Rights to Black Lives Matter, *Scientific American*, 2 February 2021

36 *Race Experts: How Racial Etiquette, Sensitivity Training, and New Age Therapy Hijacked the Civil Rights Revolution*, Elisabeth Lasch-Quinn, Rowman & Littlefield (2003)

37 College Codes Make 'Color Blindness' a Microaggression, Brendan O'Neill, *Reason*, 5 August 2015

38 University of Wisconsin-Stevens Point microaggressions, June 2015

39 Using Inclusive terminology at Mizzou, faculty diversity seminar handout, 17 July 2015

40 Color Blindness Is Counterproductive, *Atlantic*, 13 September 2015

41 Why saying 'I don't see race at all' just makes racism worse, Heather McGhee, *TED*, 3 May 2021

42 College Codes Make 'Color Blindness' a Microaggression, Brendan O'Neill, *Reason*, 5 August 2015

43 *The Silent War: Imperialism and the Changing Perception of Race*, Frank Furedi, Pluto Press (1998)

44 New Hampshire Is Too White To Have the First Primary In the Country, Democratic National Committee Chairman Says, *New Boston Post*, 15 February 2021

45 The Justice Department Is Way Too White, *New Republic*, 8 February 2021

46 BBC chief admits Monty Python wouldn't be commissioned today because it's 'too white and too Oxbridge', *Sun*, 20 June 2018

47 Healing from Toxic Whiteness: The woman behind a course helping white people tackling internalised racism, *Independent*, 23 February 2017

48 The Short Life And Death Of A 'Toxic White Progressives' List, *Buzzfeed*, 15 December 2020

49 *Black Women's Intellectualism and Deconstructing Donald Trump's Toxic White Masculinity*, Rachel Alicia Griffin, Routledge (2018)

50 *Nice Racism: How Progressive White People Perpetuate Racial Harm*, Robin DiAngelo, Beacon Press (2021)

51 Whites will always be racist, author says at Tulsa event, OCPA, 26 April 2021

52 Classical Music's Suicide Pact, Heather Mac Donald, *City Journal*, Summer 2021

53 Classical Music's Suicide Pact, Heather Mac Donald, *City Journal*, Summer 2021

54 Museums, neutrality and invisible whiteness, Museums Association

55 Museums Change Their Approach to Showing White Male Artists, *New York Times*, 27 April 2022

56 Yale English students call for end of focus on white male writers, *Guardian*, 1 June 2016

57 Universities drop Chaucer and Shakespeare as 'decolonisation' takes root, *Daily Telegraph*, 27 August 2022

58 Decolonise science – time to end another imperial era, *Conversation*, 5 April 2018

59 Decolonizing Science Means Taking Indigenous Knowledge Seriously, Dina Lupin, *This View of Life*

60 Racial Microaggressions in Everyday Life, Columbia University

7

THE LOVE THAT DARE NOT SPEAK ITS NAME

We tend to think of campus censorship as a modern curse. As the handiwork of pampered millennials brought up to believe that any utterance or idea that offends them must be extinguished. As a consequence of the 21st-century cult of self-esteem that tells the young to protect their feelings by any means necessary from the pangs of alternative thinking. In truth, campus intolerance has a long history. Academic crusades against the objectionable and profane have been taking place for decades, centuries in fact. Indeed, the magazine that first published one of the most famous lines in modern British poetry was an early victim of campus repression, some 130 years ago.

That magazine was the *Chameleon*. The poet was Lord Alfred Douglas. The line was: 'I am the love that dare not speak its name.'[1] That moving poetic cry is instantly recognisable today as a euphemism for homosexuality. Lord Douglas, known as Bosie, was the sometime lover of Oscar Wilde. They first met in 1891 when Douglas was a 21-year-old student at Oxford and Wilde a 37-year-old married father-of-two. They started an affair that would scandalise London and lead eventually to Wilde's downfall. At Wilde's trial for homosexual offences in 1895, at which he faced 25 counts of gross indecency, Douglas's poem was brought up by the prosecution. Poetry was wielded as proof of Wilde's wickedness, evidence of his engagement in illicit loves and sinful acts.

But even before the arrest and trial of Wilde, Bosie's poem and the magazine it appeared in had caused the Victorian era's guardians of morality to reach for their smelling salts. The *Chameleon* was a student journal published at Oxford University in 1894. It was expressly gay-themed, modelled on principles of Greek love, its subtitle hinting at the moral unruliness within – *A Bazaar of Dangerous and Smiling Chances*. The editor was John Francis Bloxam, an undergraduate at Exeter College, Oxford. The first issue – which transpired to be the only issue – published Wilde's 'Phrases and Philosophies for the Use of the Young'. The phrases included one of his most famous: 'To love oneself is the beginning of a lifelong romance.' And then there was Douglas's poem, titled 'Two Loves'.[2]

The *Chameleon* horrified the virtuous. Jerome K Jerome denounced it as 'garbage and offal'. It is 'an insult to the animal creation', he thundered, full of the writings of men who are 'cursed with… unnatural cravings'. Were this devilish journal to fall into the hands of an impressionable 'poor fellow', it might 'utterly ruin him for all eternity', said Jerome. 'Let us have liberty, but this is unbridled licence', he declared.[3]

When Wilde sued Douglas's father, the Marquess of Queensberry, for libel in 1895, after the Marquess called him a sodomite, the *Chameleon* came up in the trial. It was held up as proof of the correctness of the Marquess's accusations. That journal, and in particular Wilde's camp, decadent list of phrases, was evidence, the court was told, of Wilde's dream of 'corrupting the nation's youth'.[4] So great was the public scandal over the things that came to light in Wilde's libel suit against the Marquess, in particular the revelation that there existed at Oxford an openly homosexual magazine, that the publishers of the magazine felt compelled to publicly denounce it. In a letter in the *Daily Telegraph*, a lawyer for the publishing company that printed the *Chameleon* pleaded: 'We ask you to be good enough to allow us to say, through your columns, that our clients of their own act stopped the sale directly they were aware of the contents of the magazine.'[5]

And so the *Chameleon* was no more. It had been cancelled, to use modern parlance. Newspaper outrage, scandalous court proceedings and the authorities at Oxford University, desperate to quench the controversy, made sure of that. Such an act of homophobic censure would never happen today, right? Yes, that 19th-century instance of cancel culture contained many of the ingredients of modern campus crusades against dangerous ideas and materials. For example, the idea that liberty is one thing but 'unbridled licence' another – this finds expression in today's insistence that free speech has limits, that it's fine to express yourself so long as you don't go too far, aren't too offensive and never, ever cross the line into 'hate speech'. And the notion that immoral publications might ruin 'for eternity' any suggestible soul that encounters them is rehabilitated in the 21st-century ideology of the Safe Space, zones in which students can seek refuge from 'conflict, criticism or potentially threatening actions, ideas or conversations'.[6] That is, where they can hide themselves and their fragile souls from the threat of ruination posed by difficult or scandalous thinking.

But a homosexual magazine crushed underfoot? A journal celebrating same-sex love chased off campus? Surely such a stern, stiff act of intolerance, such an old-fashioned effort to protect the young from the themes of homosexuality, would never happen on the modern campus, where students and professors alike are far more relaxed about sex than were their predecessors in the Victorian era.

I wouldn't be so sure. I am not convinced a magazine like the *Chameleon* would survive any better in the era of political correctness than it did in the era of Victorian morality. Today, it would run the risk of being damned not as an 'offence against the animal creation', but as an offence against gender ideology. Today, the charge made against it would not be that it contained 'unnatural cravings', but that it implicitly contained bigoted beliefs – in particular, the bigoted belief that biological sex is more important than gender identity. Today, it would be condemned not for its corruption of young men's souls, but for the harm that its emphasis on sex, on *same-sex* love, might cause to trans people and the trans idea.

For here is one of the most striking things about the latest manifestation of political correctness, the most recent churn of this ever-shifting, ever-expanding ideology of linguistic control: it is breathing life back into homophobic thought. Some refer to it as 'woke homophobia'.[7] The problem with homosexuality, in the eyes of many modern LGBTQ crusaders, is that it emphasises a person's biological sex, hence *same-sex attraction*. And this demotes what they consider to be a far more important thing than biology – gender identity, how a person *feels* about their gender, which they might decide is entirely different to their sex. Even homosexuality has become problematic in the hysterical swirl of identity politics. Not because it is an abomination against God, but because its basis in biology is offensive to those who want to shunt us into a post-biological world in which we will be liberated from pesky scientific reality and free to pick and choose our gender as we please.

As Helen Joyce, author of *Trans: When Ideology Meets Reality*, has described it, homosexuality is suspect now, because 'in acknowledging the reality of same-sex attraction' it also 'indirectly [acknowledges] the reality and importance of biological sex as a driver of attraction'. And this contradicts the 'quasi-spiritual' crusade to 'replace biological sex with gender identity', she says.[8] The homosexual is offensive because in only feeling attracted to people of the same sex, he or she implicitly rejects the rules of gender identity, the modern commandment that says people are whatever gender they say they are. So the lesbian that feels no attraction to a man who identifies as a woman – on the basis that he is male – is a living, breathing affront to gender ideology. She is inherently transphobic. Her refusal to accept that this man who identifies as a woman really is a woman is sacrilege, a thoughtcrime against one of the key religious mantras of the identitarian era: 'Trans women are women.' Her sexual preference for women – not trans women, not men, but women – is an intolerable defiance of that mantra. Her homosexuality is bigotry. Her innate being is an outrage against the new dogmas of identitarian thought.

Same-sex attraction really is being redefined as bigotry. New slurs have emerged to brand and insult homosexuals. As a columnist for the *National Post* says, efforts have been made to 'brand homosexuality as a "genital fetish"'.[9] Kathleen Stock, a philosopher and lesbian, describes an experience where she was pointing out that lesbianism is the love of women for women, not for men, even when men identify as women, when someone said to her: 'What is this genital fetish?'[10] A BBC investigation spoke to young lesbians who said they had been branded 'genital fetishists' for refusing to sleep with 'trans women' who have penises. One was told that she owes it to her 'trans sisters' to 'unlearn my "genital confusion"'.[11] In short, learn to love penises, learn to take dick. This rehabilitates the old homophobic prejudice that lesbians just need a good 'seeing to', that that will sort them out.

Dr Veronica Ivy, a former competitive cyclist turned author on trans issues, has openly said that '"genital preferences" are transphobic'.[12] In other words, sex-based attraction is transphobic. Homosexuality is bigotry. Lesbianism is hate. Homosexuals who reject people of the opposite sex genuinely run the risk of being thought prejudiced. As a writer for the *Observer* says, '[We] are in the extraordinary position where lesbians are now being told by some activists that it is bigoted for them to say they are not attracted to trans women who are biologically male'.[13]

Even the UK's largest LGBTQ charity, Stonewall, now seems to believe that same-sex attraction can sometimes be a borderline hate crime. Yes, 'sexuality is personal', it says (very gracious), 'but if, when dating, you are writing off entire groups like people of colour or trans people, it's worth considering how societal prejudices may have shaped your attraction'.[14] Let's leave aside the cynical inclusion of people of colour alongside trans people, the low aim of which is to liken homosexuals who dare to criticise gender ideology to racists.

The more important point is that even Stonewall seems no longer to understand what homosexuality is. Of course lesbians and gay men 'write off entire groups' when they are dating. That's because they are not attracted to people of the opposite sex. For a lesbian to refuse to date a 'woman with a penis' or a gay man to refuse to sleep with a 'man with a vagina' is not proof that they have been infected by 'societal prejudices' – *it's homosexuality*.

Homosexuality risks being redefined out of existence. Stonewall was founded in 1989 to combat Section 28 of the Local Government Act of 1988, which forbade schools from 'promoting homosexuality' – that is, same-sex attraction. Yet now Stonewall avoids all talk of 'same-sex'. Instead it defines a homosexual as 'someone who has a romantic and / or sexual orientation towards someone of the same *gender*' (my emphasis).[15] But then Stonewall describes as 'transphobic' any 'denial [or] refusal to accept someone else's gender identity'. So if homosexuality is attraction on the basis of gender, but it's bigotry to question a person's professed gender, that must mean homosexuals are expected to feel attracted to anyone who claims to be the same sex as they are, even if they aren't really. As Joyce says, the 'logical consequence of these distorted definitions is to define same-sex attraction as bigotry'. In the past, it was 'conservative homophobes' who claimed that 'homosexuality was a dangerous, counterfeit identity', says Joyce: now that's done by the 'progressives running organisations that claim to champion the interests of lesbians and gay men'.[16]

Author Ben Appel captures well the internecine tumult in gay identity politics that helped to give rise to what he refers to as 'The New Homophobia'. In a piece in *Newsweek*, he described securing an internship at a major LGBTQ-rights organisation in the US in 2017. But his 'excitement about the internship quickly gave way to a nauseating mixture of fear and shame' as he clocked that his coworkers were obsessed with paving the way 'for a new generation of "queer", one that had very little to do with sex-based rights and more to do with abolishing the concepts of sex and sexuality altogether'. These queer agitators view the old homosexual guard as 'privileged and unevolved [relics] of the past', far too obsessed with the oppressive category of biological sex. The queers believe that 'subverting [these] categorisations which have been imposed upon young people – for example, the sex they were "assigned" at birth – is the ultimate expression of autonomy'. And so queer theory erases the 'oppressions' of biology and the unjust categorisations of sex, and in the process delegitimises homosexuality, too, by treating it as an archaic, sex-based category adhered to by genital fetishists and biological bigots. This is the 'new homophobia', says Appel, and 'it is threatening our very existence'.[17]

This warped new way of thinking, this likening of a homosexual's rejection of opposite-sex relations to a 'societal prejudice', even to racism, has awful real-world consequences. The younger generation has been educated via the drip drip of right-on messaging online to view same-sex attraction as bigotry. As Appel says, 'With the proliferation of social media, which disseminates ideological dogma faster than any religious institution in history, academics-cum-activists can reduce [queer theories] into palatable, easy-to-digest-and-regurgitate maxims, especially on platforms like Twitter, Tumblr and now TikTok'.[18] It isn't surprising that in such a climate, such a newly, strangely homophobic climate, more and more young people who would traditionally have identified as gay or lesbian are putting themselves forward for hormonal treatment and in some cases bodily surgery. After all, if same-sex attraction is bigotry, proof of contamination by 'societal prejudice', why not have it corrected, cured, by 'changing sex'? Then you'll be free to enjoy 'same-gender' attraction, which is good, rather than 'same-sex' attraction, which is a genital fetish.

Former employees of gender-identity clinics have likened trans treatment to 'conversion therapy for gay children'. They fear that the new homophobia is 'driving the surge in transgender young people'.

Clinicians who worked at the National Health Service's Gender Identity Development Service in London say they 'frequently had cases where people started identifying as trans after months of horrendous bullying for being gay'. Young lesbians in particular seem to view trans treatment as a corrective for their undesired sexuality. One clinician says: 'We heard a lot of homophobia… A lot of the girls would come in and say, "I'm not a lesbian. I fell in love with my best girl friend but then I went online and realised I'm not a lesbian, I'm a boy. Phew."'[19] The religious right seeks to 'pray the gay away' – gender ideologues want to drug it away. For all the criticisms one might make of hardline Christians who believe the young can be converted out of their homosexuality, at least they don't subject distressed young lesbians to hormonal interventions that break their voices and give them facial hair and to the surgical removal of their breasts. At least they only pray rather than mutilate.

The new gender ideology says that some young men are really women, locked in the biological prison of maleness. They might present, outwardly, as men, but they possess a 'female brain'.[20] It says some young women are really men, in their souls, but their flesh encasement has betrayed them, betrayed their true self, and cursed them with the visage of womanhood. In the words of a report published in the *New Scientist*, in some young women the 'white matter' in parts of their brain 'resemble[s] a male brain'.[21] Leaving to one side the question of when it became acceptable again to examine the brains of young people who are very likely homosexual – for strange matter, glitches, defects – the larger point here is that these claims of mismatching between a person's gendered soul and their meaty frame directly echo 19th-century views of 'the homosexual problem'.

Karl Heinrich Ulrichs, the German jurist and writer sometimes described as 'the first gay man in world history' for his campaigning for sexual reform in Hanover in the 1860s and 1870s, challenged the view of homosexuality as a sin by positing instead that it was a biological fault. He argued that male homosexuality was a 'congenital variation' in which a 'female soul inhabits a male body'.[22] Psychiatry embraced this defensive view of male homosexuality as female entrapment in male physicality and began to refer to homosexuality as an 'inversion', a 'reversal of the appropriate sex-role identity'.[23] The great shift had occurred, from homosexual acts being viewed as sinful and punishable to male homosexuality being treated, from the late 19th century through to the mid-20th century, as a 'congential' complication, proof of trapped femaleness or general psychological degeneration, or possibly both.

It is remarkable, and not a little disturbing, that that pre-gay-rights vision of the male homosexual as a girlish soul held hostage by male anatomy has been resuscitated by the new gender thinking. And that our supposedly enlightened societies go even further than the psychiatrists of the late 19th century and do not seek merely to treat or suppress a person's trapped true gender, but rather make the case for radically altering a person's body so that his or her physical reality better accords with their 'brain sex', as experts now say instead of 'female soul'.[24]

When it comes to encouraging people who are very likely homosexual to undergo radical surgery in order to better blend their inner gender and their outer biology, Western societies are actually behind the curve. Another society has been medically fixing the problem of gay men's trapped femaleness for far longer. It's Iran. Iran is second only to Thailand in the number of transgender surgeries it carries out.[25] And of course the reason Iran sanctions these surgeries, and even celebrates them, is not because it is trans-friendly, in thrall to the new gender ideologies that now swish around everywhere from *Teen Vogue* to TikTok. No, it's because it is a virulently homophobic society. Iran's Islamic Penal Code of 2013 forbids same-sex activity, for both men and women. The ultimate punishment is death. The trans fad in Iran is fuelled by a disgust for homosexuality so profound that the theocracy prefers lesbians to be surgically turned into 'men' and male homosexuals to be surgically turned into 'women'. Thus are they cured.

Ayatollah Khomeini himself issued a fatwa as far back as 1967, when he was in exile, expressly stating that sex-change surgeries were permissible. He issued an appendage to this fatwa in 1985 when he was in power. The theocratic justification for 'sex reassignment' is creepily similar to the arguments of modern gender ideologues in the West. *Diagnosing Identities, Wounding Bodies*, a 2014 report published by Justice for Iran, summarises it well. The ayatollahs believe that if people display 'a marked aversion to the normative mannerisms of the gender they have been assigned at birth', then they 'must undergo sex-reassignment surgeries in order to successfully uncover the truth about their sex and make it agree with their "true gender"'.[26] The ayatollahs should write an op-ed for the *Guardian*. Their determination to transform the bodies of gender non-conforming people so that they more accurately align with their 'true gender' is indistinguishable – give or take a few references to Allah and the Koran – from the cries of trans activists and their legion allies in politics and the media in the 21st-century West.

We are witnessing the re-pathologisation of homosexuality. The American Psychiatric Association described homosexuality as a 'psychiatric disorder' right up to 1973. Prior to that, it was considered a moral sickness. So the *Chameleon* was judged full of 'the cravings of an unnatural disease'.[27] Homosexuality was frequently *treated*. Alan Turing, in 1952, was subjected to the indignity of the attempted hormonal remedying of his homosexuality. Convicted of indecency, he was given a choice between jail or probation, only the probation was to be conditional on his undergoing hormonal therapy that would amount to chemical castration. He opted for the injections. They contained a synthetic oestrogen that feminised his body, rendering him impotent and giving him breasts.[28] If this sounds familiar, chillingly so, it's because the same thing is done today to teenage boys who, in another era, would simply have grown up to be gay. What we view as an abomination in the life of Turing – his subjection to a regime of hormones to correct his homosexuality – we now celebrate in the lives of young gay men. As Ben Appel says in relation to the American experience of transgenderism, these kids, the 'vast majority' of whom would have gone on to be 'gay, lesbian or bisexual in adulthood', are 'given drugs to block their puberty, cross-sex hormones and irreversible surgeries, all the while cheered on first by online communities, then the mainstream media and now the current presidential administration'.[29] Curing homosexuality is good now.

So, no – I'm not convinced a magazine like the *Chameleon* would escape censure today. I'm not convinced a publication celebrating homosexual love would be nodded through by the protectors of correct thought. It would possibly find itself condemned for its genital fetishism, denounced for the societal prejudices of its contributors who are interested only in same sex, not same gender. Maybe that love shouldn't speak its name after all. Indeed, Owen Jones, a columnist for the *Guardian*, had the following to say in relation to recent controversies over the language of same-sex attraction vs same-gender attraction: 'A gay man… might not ever [have] sex with a trans man, through circumstance or choice. He doesn't have to also declare to the world, "I won't sleep with trans men because they're really women and imposters!"… how does it impinge on his happiness not to say this?'[30]

Doesn't this sound a little like the love that dare not speak its name? Do not baldly state that you are only attracted to people of the same sex. Keep it to yourself. It will cause you no harm or hardship, gay men, to stay silent about the fact that you are attracted to men only – not to women, including women who claim to be men; just men. I'm sure it was not Jones' intention, but it does feel like we're back to Bosie. Back to the love that must keep quiet.

We need to talk about how this happened. How we went from the 1970s era of gay liberation, and the decriminalisation of homosexuality across the Western world, to a situation where even leading LGBTQ charities struggle to say it's okay to be gay, that it's okay to be attracted to people of your own sex. How we arrived in a world where not insignificant numbers of young people are submitting themselves to a 21st-century version of bodily mortification, punishing and transforming their flesh for its sins of lesbianism and male homosexuality. How we landed upon such madness that now lesbians who attend a Pride event with a banner saying 'Lesbians don't like penises' can be booed and jeered and then escorted away by the police, as happened in Cardiff in August 2022. There is 'no place for hate' in our society, said Gian Molinu, the head of Welsh Pride, about those lesbians. About that banner. About that public declaration of something that would have been considered so blindingly obvious just a few years ago that it wouldn't have needed saying, but which is now considered hate speech, the perverted cry of fetishists obsessed with vaginas.

In part, this neo-homophobia is an accomplishment of intolerance. The ideologies of political correctness advance, always, by the suppression of dissent. And in this case dissent has been well and truly suppressed. Witness the extraordinary persecutions the LGB Alliance has been subjected to for its profane insistence that homosexuality is same-sex attraction and is distinct from transgenderism and other modern forms of queer play.

The LGB Alliance was founded in 2019 by elders of the British gay-liberation movement who are concerned about the threat posed to homosexual rights by the new ideologies of gender. About the 'transing' – that is, surgical conversion – of young gay people. About the introduction of gender self-ID laws that would allow men to become women, and women to become men, simply by declaring themselves as such, and about how this might impact on the freedom of association of male homosexuals and female homosexuals. And about the wholesale erasure of the language of 'same-sex attraction', and the propensity of such authoritarian linguistic shifts to undermine the rights of homosexuals and even their ability to *argue* for their rights.

After all, as we've seen, where language is controlled, thought is controlled. One's capacity to think certain thoughts is limited and sometimes stopped entirely by the manipulation of language. This is why the semantic shift from 'same-sex' to 'same-gender' matters – it shrinks the sexual imagination, even the ability of the homosexual to understand him or herself. How is a young homosexual expected to express his or her identity, his or her desires, if the language for such things no longer exists? How can one speak of homosexual love if the words are no longer there? We've gone from the love that dare not speak its name to the love that *cannot* speak its name.

For saying these things, the LGB Alliance has been monstered by gender ideologues and the liberal media. It is branded a 'hate group', a hawker of bigotry.[31] Petitions have been launched to deprive it of Lottery funding, to demand that the UK Charity Commission rescind its charitable status. Indeed, trans-youth charity Mermaids went so far as to take legal action to appeal the awarding of charitable status to the LGB Alliance.[32] The court case involved some staggering scenes, including LGB Alliance co-founder Kate Harris being asked whether someone with a penis can be a lesbian. Harris broke down in tears at this line of questioning. When she recomposed herself, she said: 'I'm going to speak for millions of lesbians around the world who are lesbians because we love other women… We will not be erased and we will not have any man with a penis tell us he's a lesbian because he feels he is.'[33] It is a testament to PC's resuscitation of homophobic thought that a lesbian can be compelled in court to defend lesbianism. Wilde was interrogated in the dock on the love that dare not speak its name. Now lesbians are interrogated on the love that is apparently hate in disguise – women's love for other women.

The quelling of dissent explains how neo-homophobia was facilitated. How it was forced through by the deplatforming, defunding and delegitimising of those who know and fear the consequences of presenting same-sex attraction as a problem. Once again, social regression abetted by the menaces of censorship. But then there's the question of what this turn against homosexuality represents, what it tells us about our times. To my mind, the trials of homosexuality in the 21st century speak to one of the deepest moral crises of our era: the crisis of the ideal of liberation; the crisis of the belief that it is for each individual to decide for him or herself, with freedom and confidence, on how to live and who to love.

That was the principle that guided the movement for gay liberation, and other liberation movements of the modern era. Yet of late, this principle of the free life has fallen into grave disrepair. It has been slowly repealed by the ascendancy of its opposite: the therapeutic, technocratic vision of the individual as a diminished being, inefficient in reason, unwise in his choices and always requiring the guidance of health professionals, medical experts, lifestyle advisers and others who make up the new feudalism of social oversight. The dismantling of the age of liberation and its replacement with the age of intervention has led us inexorably from the old figure of the confident, liberated homosexual to today's morass of sexual and gender bewilderment that requires experts to step in to offer their diagnoses and their treatments.

One of the most important cries of the gay-liberation movement of the 1970s was against the medicalisation of homosexuality. Resistance to medicalisation was found among other groups, too, including feminism, which rejected the treatment of women for 'hysteria', and the broader anti-psychiatry movement. When the American Psychiatric Association finally voted to depathologise homosexuality, in 1973, one gay-liberation group called it 'the greatest gay victory' to date.[34] Another, mockingly, thanked the APA for cleansing gays 'of our dark and horrible sickness'.[35] The gay liberationists' rejection of pathology gave voice to a deeper rejection of authority, to a radical new belief that homosexuality did not even have to be explained, far less treated; it just was. For the first time in history, the liberty of the homosexual to live by his own choosing was to take precedence over the analyses and decrees of others. No longer sexual deviants, just people.

That era of liberation has now ended. We've seen it coming. The AIDS crisis was the first stage in the re-medicalisation of homosexuality, with gay sex being slowly brought back into the purview of the expert classes, the new issuers of advice on how men in particular should conduct themselves in the private sexual realm. Post-AIDS we witnessed the rise of the defensive plea, 'I was born this way', and the embrace of the idea of the 'gay gene'. This spoke to a creeping culture of uncertainty in the gay movement, to its inability to say what many in the recent past had said: we are. Now, the project of gay liberation, and of social liberation across the board, has almost completely surrendered to the reign of specialised expertise. Everyone seems to welcome medicalisation these days, of everything from our anxiety to our stress to our gender hang-ups. Everyone seems to accept the need for experts and gurus to guide us through life's difficulties. Everyone seems to see therapeutic governance as an essential feature of late capitalism, necessary for the management of the masses' emotions and fears. It is entirely unsurprising that, in such a moment, sexuality would come to be re-pathologised, too, returned unto the rule of the medical elites. Of brain experts, surgeons, clinicians. The 'greatest gay victory' has been undone. Sexuality has been restored as pathology. Your minds will be examined, your gender ailments diagnosed, your bodies possibly altered.

In the absence of the ideal of gay liberation, the things that gay liberation guarded against have returned. That includes medicalisation, and it includes homophobia, too. Only today the homosexual is feared less for the supposed menace he poses to family life and the social order than for the affront he represents to the pathologies of gender identity that are now in the ascendant.

Today's liberated homosexual is an outrage less against the animal creation than against the new order of gender ideology, and the new religion of gendered souls, and the authority of the high priests and their footsoldiers who oversee and enforce these post-sex, post-truth dogmas. The homosexual remains a sexual heretic.

Back to that most famous and tragic sexual heretic: Wilde. Interrogated during his trial for gross indecency about that line of Bosie's – 'the love that dare not speak its name' – he did not baulk. He argued, guardedly, that it was a reference to Platonic love, not homosexual love. But he nonetheless made a stirring case for the right to love:

> '"The love that dare not speak its name" in this century is such a great affection of an elder for a younger man as there was between David and Jonathan, such as Plato made the very basis of his philosophy, and such as you find in the sonnets of Michelangelo and Shakespeare. It is that deep, spiritual affection that is as pure as it is perfect. It dictates and pervades great works of art. It is in this century misunderstood, so much misunderstood that it may be described as "the love that dare not speak its name", and on account of it I am placed where I am now. It is beautiful, it is fine, it is the noblest form of affection. There is nothing unnatural about it.'

The court broke into applause. Some wept. It is thought by some that Wilde sealed his fate with these words, for who else but a homosexual could speak so movingly about love between men? If he did damn himself, at least he did so while defending what he believed to be true, and while standing up for love, which is something we might take heart from in these harsh and conformist times.

1 'Two Loves', Lord Alfred Douglas, 1894

2 *Chameleon*, Issue 1, 1894

3 *The Secret Life of Oscar Wilde*, Neil McKenna, Arrow (2004)

4 *Love in Earnest: Some Notes on the Lives and Writings of English 'Uranian' Poets from 1889 to 1930*, Timothy d'Arch Smith, Routledge (1970)

5 *Love in Earnest: Some Notes on the Lives and Writings of English 'Uranian' Poets from 1889 to 1930*, Timothy d'Arch Smith, Routledge (1970)

6 Merriam Webster

7 Meet the Gay Activists Who've Had Enough of Britain's Ultra-Woke Homophobes, Helen Joyce, *Quillette*, 11 April 2019

8 Meet the Gay Activists Who've Had Enough of Britain's Ultra-Woke Homophobes', Helen Joyce, *Quillette*, 11 April 2019

9 Emerging woke homophobia shows how progressives demand conformity, Adam Zivo, *National Post*, 23 June 2022

10 Of course sex materially exists, kathleenstock.com, 18 June 2020

11 The lesbians who feel pressured to have sex and relationships with trans women, BBC News, 26 October 2021

12 The lesbians who feel pressured to have sex and relationships with trans women, BBC News, 26 October 2021

13 If a lesbian only desires same-sex dates that's not bigotry, it's her right, Sonia Sodha, *Observer*, 29 May 2022

14 The lesbians who feel pressured to have sex and relationships with trans women, BBC News, 26 October 2021

15 List of LGBTQ+ terms, stonewall.org.uk

16 Meet the Gay Activists Who've Had Enough of Britain's Ultra-Woke Homophobes, Helen Joyce, *Quillette*, 11 April 2019

17 The New Homophobia, Ben Appel, *Newsweek*, 21 April 2022

18 The New Homophobia, Ben Appel, *Newsweek*, 21 April 2022

19 It feels like conversion therapy for gay children, say clinicians, *The Times*, 8 April 2019

20 Is There Something Unique about the Transgender Brain?, *Scientific American*, 1 January 2016

21 Transsexual differences caught on brain scan, *New Scientist*, 26 January 2011

22 *Origins of Sexuality and Homosexuality*, John De Cecco and Michael Shively, Taylor & Francis (2014)

23 *Origins of Sexuality and Homosexuality*, John De Cecco and Michael Shively, Taylor & Francis (2014)

24 Brain Sex in Transgender Women Is Shifted towards Gender Identity, *Journal of Clinical Medicine*, March 2022

25 'Everyone treated me like a saint'– In Iran, there's only one way to survive as a transgender person, Neha Thirani Bagri, *QZ*, 19 April 2017

26 *Diagnosing Identities, Wounding Bodies: Medical Abuses and Other Human Rights Violations Against Lesbian, Gay and Transgender People in Iran*, Justice for Iran, 2014

27 *Love in Earnest: Some Notes on the Lives and Writings of English 'Uranian' Poets from 1889 to 1930*, Timothy d'Arch Smith, Routledge (1970)

28 Alan Turing's Body, *Atlantic*, 26 December 2013

29 The New Homophobia, Ben Appel, *Newsweek*, 21 April 2022

30 Owen Jones, Twitter, 15 September 2022

31 LGB Alliance: Anti-trans lobby group's troubling, ugly history, *Pink News*, 14 September 2022

32 Gay rights group was set up 'to promote transphobic activity', court told, *Guardian*, 12 September 2022

33 LGB Alliance co-founder breaks down in court when asked to define 'lesbian', *Guardian*, 15 September 2022

34 We Are Certain of Our Own Insanity: Antipsychiatry and the Gay Liberation Movement, 1968–1980, *Journal of the History of Sexuality*, January 2016

35 We Are Certain of Our Own Insanity: Antipsychiatry and the Gay Liberation Movement, 1968–1980, *Journal of the History of Sexuality*, January 2016

8

VIVA HATE

I've been thinking about what we might call the paradox of hate. This is the curious fact that we live in societies that are preoccupied with policing and punishing hatred and yet hatred abounds. It flourishes. Hate is the *lingua franca* of social media. The dictionary of hate grows fatter by the week. New spiteful slurs are always emerging. Gammon, TERF, Tory scum, coconut (for Tory scum who are also black). These barbs drip with contempt. They rip the humanity from their targets. Every day on the internet there's a Two Minutes Hate. That 'hideous ecstasy of fear and vindictiveness' that grips Party members in *Nineteen Eighty-Four* as they are excited into a frenzy of hate is everywhere now. For us, as for them, hate flows through the mob 'like an electric current'. Twittermobs are marshalled, insults are hurled. Die TERF. Delete your account. Kill Tory scum.[1] Kill yourself. It's hate upon hate.

And here's the burning core of the paradox of hate: much of this loathing, much of this molten contempt for the other, comes from the kind of people who say they oppose 'hate speech'. From the kind of people who, in any other setting, when they aren't raging against those witches who criticise the ideology of transgenderism or those black Tories who have sold out their race for a taste of power, will be found shaking their heads over the scourge of 'hate speech' and 'hate crime'.

Consider the case of JK Rowling. Few public figures are subjected to as much bile and menace as she is. Her crime is well known: she thinks men are not women. She thinks a man never becomes a woman, despite how many pills he pops or surgeries he undergoes. Her heresy is to understand biology. For that she is insulted and threatened daily. And the insults come from the kind of people who have the Pride flag in their social-media bios, and who say 'Love is Love', and who loudly lament the hate speech of transphobia, and who will be on the phone to the cops to report a 'hate crime' if someone makes the mistake of misgendering them faster than you can say 'what a hypocrite'. They take noisy public stands against hate speech and then they engage in hate speech, submitting themselves to the twisted delights and delirium of visiting hate upon the great she-devil of the 21st century. That's the paradox.

The hate for Rowling really is intense. She's branded a TERF, of course, which literally means 'trans-exclusionary radical feminist', but which really means insubordinate, possibly hysterical woman who outrageously refuses to bow before the ideology of transgenderism.

Rowlingphobia swirls through social media. 'Kill yourself.' 'Bitch I'll murder you.' 'Die bitch.' 'This woman is complete scum.' 'Shut the fuck up.' 'I will beat the fuck out of you.' All of that has been said to Rowling. And worse. She's regularly threatened with death, with that ultimate punishment for her sins of biological belief. Her home address was posted on Twitter alongside an image of a bomb-making handbook. There's a song on YouTube about her that goes: 'I hope you fit in a hearse, bitch.' When Rowling tweeted her concern and solidarity for Salman Rushdie following his stabbing in New York in August 2022, someone replied: 'Don't worry you're next.'[2]

The most unhinged hate for Rowling is vomited up from the underbelly of the internet, of course. It's there, in that moral wasteland, that she's most often told to 'fuck off and die' or invited to 'suck my girldick'. It's there you'll see people turn into 'grimacing, screaming lunatics' possessed by 'a desire to kill, to torture, to smash faces in with a sledgehammer', *à la* Orwell's Two Minutes Hate. Yet these people's fits of detestation are unquestionably inflamed by the mainstream media's acceptance of the idea that Rowling's dissent on transgenderism does indeed make her 'phobic', which is to say hateful, which is to say dangerous, which is to say *a bitch*.

Headlines like 'Daniel Radcliffe talks JK Rowling's transphobic comments' and 'Where JK Rowling's anti-trans views come from' and 'JK Rowling and anti-trans rhetoric have caused "significant damage" to the UK' throw the fuel of legitimation on to the fires of Rowlingphobia. When outlets as mainstream as NBC News report the view that Rowling is 'literally harming the trans community' and that she is promoting 'hate-crime messages against the trans community', it isn't surprising that others come to hate her.[3] When Mermaids, the trans-youth charity, says Rowling might even unwittingly be causing people to die ('there have been cases of self-harm and even attempted suicide [among trans youths] following JK Rowling's statements'), it is hardly surprising that some start to see her as a threat, even to themselves personally.[4] Her words have caused 'significant damage' to Britain? They make young trans people want to end their lives? What a bitch. Ready the hearse. It is a short journey indeed from the mainstream idea that Rowling's belief in biological sex is a phobic ideology that causes harm and illness and possibly death to the extremist cry that this woman is complete scum whose life must end.

Then there's the puzzle at the heart of all of this, and at the heart of the broader hate debate today. Which is that all the violent scorn for Rowling is coming from a movement – the trans movement – that is myopically obsessed with correct speech, with promoting what it thinks of as good, nice, respectful terminology. A movement that implores and even works with officialdom to cleanse hateful words from the public arena. They hate hate, except their own.

Trans activists and their allies see hate speech everywhere. Misgendering is hate speech in their eyes – that's when you refer to a biological male as 'he' when he now claims to be a 'she'. TikTok's definition of hate speech was updated in 2022, under pressure from trans activists, to include misgendering as an unutterable offence.[5]

'Deadnaming' too – that's when you say out loud a trans person's old name, their birth name. That's like saying Voldemort in woke circles, if they'll forgive the Rowling analogy: it's dangerous speech that might bring forth evil. Misgendering is an expression of a hateful ideology, says TikTok, and it is being made verboten for the 'wellbeing of our community'.[6] Misgendering is seen as damaging to people's very souls. It has 'negative consequences' for trans people's 'overall mental health', says one report.[7] So referring to a female-identifying man as 'he' is a hateful, harmful lie, but wondering out loud if JK Rowling deserves a slap is okay, at least in the eyes of some in the trans set.

Trans activists go to enormous lengths, perhaps more than any other identitarian group, to expunge 'hate' from public life. Students' unions in the UK No Platform transphobia, which has led to even Germaine Greer being threatened with censorship. More than 3,000 people signed a petition in 2015 to try to prevent Greer from delivering a lecture on women and power at Cardiff University on the basis that Greer's refusal to accept that men can become women is transphobia. In the end, the lecture went ahead, with uniformed police officers standing guard to protect the allegedly hateful Greer from assault.[8] *Cherwell*, the Oxford University student newspaper, has defended the No Platforming of 'transphobia' on the basis that transphobes are not unlike fascists. 'Fascists', it said, 'appeal to fear: fear of immigrants, fear of change, fear of moral collapse and social implosion. Trans-exclusionary radical feminists – TERFs – appeal to fear and to disgust: of the sexual other, of transitioning, of "men" perverting the female.' It used to be the alt-right that referred to feminists as fascists – 'feminazis'. Now it's the correct-thinking left. So it's fascism for a feminist to state biological facts, but it's fine for YouTube singers to wonder if that bitch Rowling will fit in their hearse. Biology is hate speech, Rowlingphobia is just speech.

Women have even been arrested for what trans activists have decreed to be their hateful words. In January 2022, a woman in

Newport in Wales was arrested for putting up stickers and posters that were said to contain 'threatening or abusive writing likely to cause harassment, alarm or distress'.[9] That is, they called into question some of the ideas of transgenderism, including the idea that trans women are women. In 2018, a woman was arrested at her home in Hertfordshire in England in part for the crime of 'misgendering' a trans person on Twitter.[10] In August 2022, a police community support officer subjected a woman to a long lecture about the wickedness of the trans-sceptical stickers she had on her front door. 'Where you are in your thinking', the officer said, 'is very much needing a lot of enlightenment and reading'.[11] This echoed the infamous questioning of Harry Miller by Humberside Police in January 2019 for the sin of liking and sharing 'anti-trans' tweets. Miller was lectured for 34 minutes by an officer who said he needed to 'check [Miller's] thinking'.[12] Thoughtpolicing is real. Political correctness has reached the highest stage of authoritarianism – the examination of the human mind itself for any unapproved idea or flicker of intellectual defiance. Even thinking wrongly on trans issues is hate, whereas witch-hunting Rowling morning, noon and night is 'activism'.

How do we explain this? This strange situation where a movement that has done as much as any other to chase 'hate speech' from the town square, to damn as shaming and painful any utterance it dislikes, has also birthed one of the most genuinely hateful crusades of modern times: the demonisation of JK Rowling? It's tempting to see it as mere hypocrisy. As a consequence of the suffocations of self-righteousness, where one always sees sin in other people's behaviour, but never in one's own. The trans set wouldn't be the first movement in history so focused on the mote in other people's eyes that it couldn't feel the beam in its own.

But there's more to it than that. That so much hate speech is expressed, or at the very least facilitated, by a movement that claims to be against hate speech is not an accident. It is not a glitch in the system. No, it is a function of the very ideology of anti-hate, of the empire of hate control and hate censorship that has grown so large and so powerful in the 21st century. We need to think afresh about the purpose of Western elites' war on hate, of their drawing up of vast tracts of legislation and workplace speech codes and police guidance to tackle what they view as the free-floating evil that is hatred. For it is not about tackling hate at all. It's about *sanctioning* hate.

The crusade against hate actually gives us a warrant to hate. It gives us a licence to loathe. Through continually indicating which ideas it is no longer acceptable for people to hold, whether that's the idea that men cannot become women or that same-sex marriage is immoral or that Islam is regressive, hate-speech strictures invite us to attack those ideas and, by extension, the people who hold them. In metaphorically marking certain beliefs with a huge red 'H' for hate, the new empire of censorship incites hatred against those beliefs. In branding certain social groups and religious groups as spreaders of the disease of hate, as 'literally harmful' to their fellow citizens, the elites' ideology of anti-hate inflames hate. You may hate the hateful; you *must*, in fact, for how else will we cleanse society of their unholy influences?

So it is no coincidence that Rowling is so feverishly hated by those who are against hate. Nor that our societies feel more cursed with hateful crusades than they have been for a very long time, in spite of the relentless rise of laws and codes against hate. For those laws and codes nurture hatred. Hate is the ironic and bastard offspring of anti-hate.

It cannot have escaped people's notice that hate has been the constant companion of the war on hate. University campuses are overrun with speech codes and Safe Spaces designed to ward off hate, yet witness the hate that will grip these selfsame student officials the minute a representative of Israel turns up at their campus. Then they'll 'throw chairs, smash windows and set off fire alarms' in one of those new hideous ecstasies of fear.[13] Liberal media outlets are forever wringing their hands over hate and yet they'll chortle when novelist Ian McEwan jokes about the deaths of old people and how beneficial those deaths will be to the country. '1.5million oldsters, mostly Brexiteers, freshly in their graves', dreamed McEwan in 2017. And what a blessed relief it will be to be rid of this 'gang of angry old men, irritable even in victory', who damned Britain with Brexit.[14] How the anti-hate set lapped it up. Don't engage in elder hate, the right-thinking warn us, yet then they're fantasising about depriving oldies of the right to vote. 'We should ban old people from voting', said a writer for *GQ* in 2016 who, like so many in the media establishment, was in the throes of grief over Brexit.[15]

Don't punch down, the PC say. Punching down – which is to have a laugh at the expense of someone less politically or culturally powerful than you – is furiously frowned on these days. And yet, as we've seen, they'll punch down till they're exhausted against that 'nest of gammon', those 'meat'-coloured lower classes, those dreadful people who resemble a 'minging cut of overly salty pork best saved for dog's dinners'. You can hate them. In fact it's virtually mandatory to hate the meat-hued masses on certain dinner-party circuits.

Racial hatred, of course, is the great sin of our times. But they'll make an exception for blacks or Asians who deviate from what they deem to be the correct way for blacks and Asians to think and behave. Consider non-white folks in the upper echelons of the Conservative Party. That lot are just 'pawn[s] in white supremacy'.[16] They're people 'with brown skin wearing Tory masks', said a piece in the *Guardian* of all places.[17] A paper that also depicted then home secretary Priti Patel as a cow with a ring through its nose.[18] So it's even acceptable in the era of anti-hate to depict non-white people as animals again. Online armies of supposedly anti-hate people will brand black Conservatives and Republicans as 'sell-outs', 'coconuts', 'Uncle Toms'.[19] When it was leaked that the Supreme Court was set to overturn *Roe v Wade*, it was the black and pro-life justice, Clarence Thomas, who got the most flak from the online mob. 'Just another dumb field nigger', 'coon-ass motherfucker', a 'nigger slave' to his 'nutcase' wife – good anti-hate progressives said those things about Thomas.[20] 'Uncle Clarence', Samuel L Jackson called him.[21] Maybe he ain't really black, as anti-hate Joe Biden once said of African-Americans who were thinking of voting for Trump.[22]

So racial hatred is bad, except the racial hatred of assuming that all ethnic-minority people must adhere to the same leftish, liberal worldview. Except the racial hatred of treating blacks and Asians as representatives of their race, rather than as individuals who are capable of deciding for themselves what to think about the world. Except the racial hatred of branding any ethnic-minority person who dares to deviate from the political narrative drawn up by mostly white liberals as a race traitor, a dumb pawn, an Uncle Tom, a coon. Witness one progressive academic's denunciation of black British broadcaster Trevor Phillips as a 'modern-day Uncle Tom' engaged in 'coonery'.[23]

On and on it swirls, the paradox of hate. Don't be misogynistic, except in relation to those bitches who don't believe men can become women. Don't be homophobic, except when it comes to those ageing queens in the LGB Alliance. Don't be classist, unless you're confronted by one of those ghastly gammon out of its nest. Don't be fatphobic, except towards those fat chavs in the Brexity parts of Britain who dragged us out of the EU. In June 2016, researchers, to the great amusement of the chattering classes, found that 'areas with high obesity levels were much more likely to vote Leave'.[24] 'Fat old racists', said one Labour MP about Leave voters.[25] Don't demonise immigrant-descended communities, except the Jews. And maybe Hindus, too. Witness the spread of the Socialism of Fools among the supposedly anti-hate British left in recent years. Or the way Britain's Hindu community is talked about as the importer of far-right ideologies, of 'chauvinistic bile' and 'poisonous ideas' and 'Hindu chauvinism'.[26] No politically correct protection from criticism for those people. Knock yourselves out, haters.

Or just think about the *culture* of discussion today. It is unforgiving. It is almost violently intolerant. Cancellation awaits those who make the merest intellectual misstep. And cancellation is always attended by hate. Cancellation *is* hate, in fact. It's a declaration that you hate a person and what he represents so very much that you are seeking his permanent and irreversible exclusion from your university, your social media, your world. It is a metaphorical execution for heresy. The person might still live, yes, but he doesn't live where you can see him. You have obliterated him. A medieval banishment, fired by hate.

Strikingly, it is among the young in particular, among those most thoroughly inculcated with the ideology of anti-hate, that social mercilessness reigns supreme. Chimamanda Ngozi Adichie captures it well. She writes about the 'cold-blooded grasping' in certain youthful circles – 'a hunger to take and take and take, but never give', 'a massive sense of entitlement', 'an ease with dishonesty and pretension and selfishness that is couched in the language of self-care', 'an astonishing level of self-absorption', 'language that is slick and sleek but with little emotional intelligence', 'a passionate performance of virtue that is well executed in the public space of Twitter, but not in the intimate space of friendship'. And, of course, 'an unrealistic expectation of puritanism from others'. They will 'demand that you denounce your friends for flimsy reasons in order to remain a member of the chosen puritan class', says Adichie. They will tell you to 'educate yourself' while 'not having actually read any books themselves'. They will 'wield the words "violence" and "weaponise" like tarnished pitchforks'. The end result? A new generation that is terrified of saying the wrong thing, of entertaining the wrong thought, lest they be 'attacked by their own'.

'The assumption of good faith is dead', says Adichie. 'What matters is not goodness but the appearance of goodness. We are no longer human beings. We are now angels jostling to out-angel one another. God help us. It is obscene.'[27]

It is obscene. It is also logical. A society that marks certain ideas and people as 'hateful' should not be surprised to find new forms of hate emerging. Hating hate is the great progressive pursuit of our time. To hate is to be virtuous now. You just have to make sure you hate the right things, the right people. Those that have had the accusation of hatefulness hung round their necks – hate them. Traditional Christians, old white men with outdated social views, gender-critical feminists, supporters of populism, people critical of mass immigration, religious opponents of same-sex marriage, intellectually disobedient black people, immigrant groups that are too successful, too 'privileged', too inclined to vote for the right. These are the ones seared with the brand of hate. These are the ones you may hate.

Hate-speech laws and hate-speech codes are best seen not as efforts by the rulers of our societies to create fairer, nicer communities, but as attempts to determine what it is acceptable for people to think and say and what it is not acceptable for people to think and say. Strictures against hate speech are really a line in the sands of morality (an ever-shifting line, it should be noted), decreeing which beliefs it is permissible for the public to hold. The European elites' long-running discussion about hate speech makes it clear that the term doesn't only refer to expressions of racism or anti-Semitism. It also refers to those thoughts the elites currently view as undesirable or incorrect, and as deserving of hate.

The definition of hate is so flabby that an utterance doesn't even have to be expressly hateful to be considered hate speech. In 2008, a factsheet produced by the European Court of Human Rights said 'the identification of expressions that could be qualified as "hate speech" is sometimes difficult because this kind of speech does not necessarily manifest itself through the expression of hatred or of emotions'.[28] Apparently, it can 'also be concealed in statements which at a first glance may seem to be rational or normal'. So ostensibly 'normal' speech, free of hate, might turn out upon closer inspection to be hate. Who makes that decision? Who divines in their infinite wisdom that a 'normal' statement is hate in drag? The European Union Agency for Fundamental Rights is vaguer still. Yes, hate speech usually refers to 'the incitement and encouragement of hatred, discrimination or hostility towards an individual that is motivated by prejudice against that person because of a particular characteristic', it says. But hate speech also 'includes a broader spectrum of verbal acts', including 'disrespectful public discourse'. So is hate speech hate or disrespect? Is it contempt for certain people or just being coarse in your chatter? Is it racism or rudeness?[29]

As Paul Coleman points out in his book *Censored: How European 'Hate Speech' Laws are Threatening Freedom of Speech*, this murky, blurry definition of hate can be seen in actual hate-speech laws, too. So, in Germany, it is an offence to commit 'an insult', where an 'insult' is defined as an 'illegal attack on the honour of another person, by intentionally showing disrespect or no respect at all'. In Greece, you can potentially be jailed for hate for showing a 'lack of respect' towards God. In Spain, even making fun of atheists, 'publicly mock[ing] those who do not profess any religion or belief', is potentially a hate offence. The subjectivity of the anti-hate ideology is most clear in the UK. Here, alongside the Public Order Act, the Malicious Communications Act and the Racial and Religious Hatred Act, all of which criminalise certain forms of hateful or harmful or alarming speech, we also have 'non-crime hate incidents'. That's any incident 'which may or may not constitute a criminal offence' but which 'is perceived by the victim or any other person as being motivated by prejudice or hate'. Any other person. Anyone at all. It is sufficient for one random individual to believe you said or did something from a position of hate for you to be branded one of the wicked ones. As Coleman says, 'perception is often reality' in the world of hate policing.

These vaguely worded laws on hate have led to the punishment or threatened punishment of thousands of people across Europe. And not just for old-fashioned race hate, but also for giving voice to moral views that the 21st-century establishment just doesn't like very much. Like the Belgian cardinal threatened with legal action for saying many gays and lesbians are 'sexual perverts'. Or the Spanish bishop briefly placed under criminal investigation for saying homosexuality is a 'defective way of expressing sexuality'. Or the woman in Austria convicted for making 'disparaging' comments about the Prophet Muhammad. Or the arrest of various street preachers in the UK for giving public expression to the Biblical view on homosexuality (it's not positive). One, in Manchester in 2011, was arrested and held in custody for 19 hours for preaching that God hates the gay sin. (He later received compensation for false imprisonment.) Or the church in rural England that was investigated by police in May 2014 for displaying a sign showing the burning fires of hell alongside the words: 'If you think there is no God, you better be right!!' A passer-by was offended, called the cops, and they recorded the sign as a 'hate incident'. In the past, heretics were told they were heading for hell – now it's heresy for Christians just to talk about hell.[30]

The recording of an actual Christian belief as a 'hate incident' confirms that anything can be considered hate these days. Any eccentric or controversial or simply unpopular view can be interpreted as a spiteful, hurtful idea that the hate-watchers have a duty to crush. Other non-crime hate incidents recorded in the UK include the aforementioned 'anti-trans' tweets posted by Harry Miller – including a limerick – and even a 2017 speech by then home secretary Amber Rudd about immigration. An Oxford professor felt offended by the speech, despite not having watched or read it, and reported it to the police, who duly logged it as a 'hate incident' alongside all the other hate incidents in their bulging book of thoughtcrimes.[31] All of the above cases pertain to people's moral and political beliefs, whether about the ungodliness of homosexuality or the wickedness of Muhammad or the unreality of transgenderism. You can agree or disagree with their takes. You can think them right or wrong or repulsive. That's your call. But we should absolutely reject the right of officialdom to criminalise moral belief as 'hate'. For one man's 'hate speech' is another man's deeply held conviction.

Harry Miller took Humberside Police to court for violating his speech rights and won. The judge said the police had 'undervalu[ed] a cardinal democratic freedom'. 'In this country we have never had a Cheka, a Gestapo or a Stasi', he said. 'We have never lived in an Orwellian society.' And yet we do now. The secular pathologisation of certain creeds and ideas as 'hate', and the punishment of them as such, represents an intolerable interference with the right to think and speak freely. It is no more legitimate to investigate hate – an emotion, a feeling – than it would be to investigate thought. The category of 'hate speech' should feel as repugnant to believers in freedom of speech as the category of thoughtcrime would. They're one and the same, in fact. That police officer who said he was 'checking [the] thinking' of Harry Miller was being brilliantly honest – hate-policing is thought-checking.

The ideology of anti-hate has trickled down into almost every area of life. Universities, workplaces, social media – all now have speech codes justified in the puffed-up lingo of stopping hate. And these non-state rules are often more expansive even than the state's. Consider social-media sites like Twitter where, pre-Musk, you could be banned for life for referring to a biological male who identifies as a woman as 'he'. Hate control in the past was about combating scourges like biological racism – now it punishes expressions of *biological facts*. This is the ever-expanding empire of emotion policing. That the war on hate has morphed and grown from the punishment of racial hatred to the online silencing of anyone who dares to utter a trans person's birth name is the clearest confirmation you could ask for that censorship is an insatiable beast. Only a fool would believe that censorship can be trained and controlled to devour only ideas he doesn't like. Once you let censorship off its leash, there is no stopping it.

We've gone from the introduction of laws against the expression of racial hatred to a situation today where a UK police force sternly warns Twitter users not to take the piss out of a paedophile. 'Sussex Police do not tolerate any hateful comments towards [a person's] gender identity regardless of crimes committed', these cops said when tweeters referred to Sally Ann Dixon, a female-identifying male child abuser, as a bloke. So there's your noble war on hate. This is where it ends. With a man who sexually abused seven children over two decades being protected from the 'hateful' indignity of being correctly called a man. Permit the authorities to punish emotion and you empower them to punish all emotion, even the emotion of loathing a paedophile.

In penalising hate, officialdom green-lights hate. The criminal pursuit of priests who don't like homosexuality, the campus censorship of gender-critical feminists, the social-media shutdown of anything the hip millionaires of Silicon Valley consider to be 'hateful' – all of this puts a target sign on certain beliefs, and on the holders of those beliefs. Under the banner of fighting hatred, the powers-that-be incite hatred. Hatred of the wrongthinker, of the traditionally religious, of the transphobe, of the blasphemer against Muhammad. Hatred of the moral deviant. Hatred of the heretic. That's what the accusation of 'hate speaker' really means – that you are a heretic, your ideas and your lifestyle an affront to the new priestly elites that police and enforce the distinction between 'normal' thinking and 'hateful' thinking.

We've been here before. This is a secular version of the Inquisition. That fiery assault on heresy was likewise fuelled by hatred for the hateful.[32] 'The perfect hatred', some inquisitors called it, from Psalms 139:21: 'Do I hate them, O Lord, that hate thee? And am not I grieved with those that rise up against thee? I hate them with perfect hatred: I count them mine enemies.'

The perfect hatred is back. The hateful urge to punish those who hate – not those who hate God, this time, but those who hate certain groups or certain ideologies – is gripping Europe once more. To these neo-Torquemadas we should bring the wisdom of that great opponent of the Inquisition, Spinoza. 'In a free state every man may think what he likes, and say what he thinks', Spinoza said. 'Government which attempts to control minds is accounted tyrannical, and it is considered an abuse of sovereignty and a usurpation of the rights of subjects.'

It is tyranny we should hate, whether religious or secular, whether justified to protect God from hate or to protect society from hate. The perfect hatred has no place in a free and civilised community.

1 We wrote 'Kill Tory Scum' in protest at brutal austerity. Glastonbury was once a haven for political dissent – what happened?, *Independent*, 3 June 2019

2 From Rushdie to Rowling – how identity politics turned violent, Brendan O'Neill, *spiked*, 15 August 2022

3 JK Rowling Receives Backlash After New Comments About the Transgender Community, NBC News, 5 July 2020

4 A Call to JK Rowling, Mermaids, 28 August 2020

5 TikTok Tightens Rules to Bar Transphobic Behaviour Such as Deadnaming, Bloomberg, 9 February 2022

6 TikTok bans misgendering, deadnaming from its content, NPR, 9 February 2022

7 What Does It Mean to Misgender Someone?, *HealthLine*, 18 September 2018

8 Germaine Greer gives university lecture despite campaign to silence her, *Guardian*, 18 November 2015

9 Newport: Nothing hateful in stickers, says arrested woman, BBC News, 27 January 2022

10 Woman arrested for misgendering a trans person on Twitter charged with trolling, *Pink News*, 5 September 2019

11 Bella Doe, Twitter, 14 August 2022

12 Humberside Police tell man to 'check his thinking' after he likes 'offensive transgender limerick' on Twitter, *Hull Daily Mail*, 25 January 2019

13 University's Israel society event is attacked by demonstrators who throw chairs and smash windows because the country's ex-secret service chief was speaking, *Daily Mail*, 20 January 2016

14 Death of '1.5m oldsters' could swing second Brexit vote, says Ian McEwan, *Guardian*, 12 May 2017

15 We should ban old people from voting, *GQ*, 14 June 2016

16 Don't Be Fooled, Priti Patel And Sajid Javid's Cabinet Appointments Do Nothing For Diversity, *Huffington Post*, 25 July 2019

17 Don't be fooled by Johnson's 'diverse' cabinet. Tory racism hasn't changed, Kehinde Andrews, *Guardian*, 25 July 2019

18 Priti Patel criticises 'racist' cartoon showing her as a 'fat cow' in the *Guardian*, *Metro*, 9 June 2020

19 Sajid Javid demands Jeremy Corbyn denounce his supporters for branding him a 'coconut' and 'Uncle Tom' since his appointment as Home Secretary, *Daily Mail*, 2 May 2018

20 Clarence Thomas and the racism of the woke elites, Brendan O'Neill, *spiked*, 26 June 2022

21 Samuel L. Jackson Calls Out 'Uncle Clarence' Thomas After Roe v. Wade Ruling, *Hollywood Reporter*, 25 June 2022

22 Biden: 'If you have a problem figuring out whether you're for me or Trump, then you ain't black', CNN, 22 May 2020

23 Kehinde Andrews, Twitter, 9 March 2020

24 UEA research claims link between obesity and Brexit voters, ITV, 30 June 2016

25 Labour MP brands Brexit voters 'fat old racists', *Spectator*, 26 August 2020

26 Who is to blame for Hindutva violence in Britain?, *Socialist Worker*, 24 September 2022

27 It is obscene: a true reflection in three parts, chimamanda.com, 15 June 2021

28 Factsheet: Hate Speech, Council of Europe, November 2008

29 See *Censored: How European 'Hate Speech' Laws are Threatening Freedom of Speech*, Paul Coleman, KAIROS Publications (2016)

30 See *Censored: How European 'Hate Speech' Laws are Threatening Freedom of Speech*, Paul Coleman, KAIROS Publications (2016)

31 Illiberal policing: it's time to abolish 'non-crime hate incidents', *Article*, 4 May 2021

32 *Holy Hatred: Christianity, Anti-Semitism and the Holocaust*, Robert Michael, Palgrave Macmillan (2006)

9

THE PRETENDERS

Meet the Pretendians. These are the white folk in the US and Canada who pretend to be Indians. Who cosplay, often for years and years, as people of indigenous heritage. Who don traditional woven cloaks and feather-based headgear and give themselves names like Morning Star Bear despite not having a drop of indigenous blood in their veins. Who loudly and proudly claim to have Cherokee or Cree or Métis origins even though they're descended from whites who got off the boat from Europe just a few decades ago. They're committing 'ethnic fraud', says one Native American writer, and there's a shocking number of them.[1]

There's Carrie Bourassa, who was a professor of community health and epidemiology at the University of Saskatchewan in Canada. She was an expert on indigenous issues as well. Or so she said. In 2019, she gave a TED talk in which she was holding a feather and wearing a vivid blue indigenous-style shawl. 'My name's Morning Star Bear', she told the audience. 'Ooh, I'm just going to say it, I'm emotional. I'm Bear Clan. I'm Anishinaabe Métis from Treaty Four Territory.'[2] The audience lapped it up, so enchanted to be in the presence of this woman whose identity seemed so much more exotic and authentic than their own. Bourassa teared up as she described being surrounded by 'the spirit of her ancestors'.[3] One of those was 'gramps', her Métis granddad, who would take her on excursions to pick berries and tan hides, she said, and who once gave her a pair of mukluks (boots made from sealskin).

There was only one problem: it was bunkum. Bourassa's Instagram page had declared to the world that she was an indigenous feminist and proud Métis with an addiction to lattes – and in the unsparing words of the *New York Post*, 'Only her penchant for caffeine was true'.[4] In 2021, she was exposed as another ethnic fraud. A group of researchers suspicious of her claims to indigenous heritage poked around in her family tree and discovered that she's actually of Swiss, Hungarian, Polish and Czech origin, with 'not one ounce of indigenous blood'.[5] She grew up in a white middle-class family. Her dad owned a car-cleaning business. Old photos show her with her bespectacled, Eastern European grandparents, nothing like that 'gramps' who supposedly took her into the wild to skin animals and make leather.

Bourassa got away with her Native Canadian version of blacking up for years. She benefitted from it enormously, winning academic clout on the basis of her indigenous claims and even rising to become the scientific director of Canada's federal Institute of Indigenous Peoples' Health. Not bad for a woman from a Swiss-Hungarian-Polish middle-class background. She stepped aside from all those influential and well-remunerated roles after her Métis scam was exposed.

Then there's Joseph Boyden, the best-selling Canadian novelist who for years claimed indigenous heritage. That claim seems to have stemmed in part from his uncle, who was a well-known Native Indian figure in Canada in the 1950s. Well, kind of. His name was 'Injun Joe' and he'd wear a headdress while selling curios from a wigwam at the entrance to Algonquin Park in Ontario. Injun Joe's real name, however, was Earl Boyden and he was the son of a 'well-to-do Ottawa merchant who traced his family to Thomas O'Boyden in Yorkshire [in England]'.[6] Even back then it was known that Injun Joe weren't no Indian. A *Maclean's* article in 1956 said this strange and entertaining man so beloved of visitors to Algonquin Park 'may look like an Indian, think like an Indian and spend most of his year among Indians, but as far as he knows he hasn't a drop of Indian blood'.[7]

Fast forward a few decades and this guy's nephew is pulling a similar stunt, though in a far more sophisticated way than by sitting in a wigwam selling Native tat to tourists. Now the Pretendians have gone respectable. They write novels and hold academic positions and give TED talks, all while claiming to be surrounded by the ghosts of their pained, wronged ancestors. So Joseph Boyden doesn't 'culturally appropriate' Native Indian headdress like his uncle Injun Joe did. No, he writes novels and books on indigenous themes. He treats 'indigenous stories as his own', his critics argue, and 'gain[s] fame and fortune from doing so'.[8]

The 21st-century Injun Joes are everywhere. Even Sacheen Littlefeather, one of the best-known Native Americans of recent decades, seems to have been a Pretendian. Littlefeather's global fame stemmed from the time Marlon Brando sent her in his place to collect his Best Actor gong for *The Godfather* at the 1973 Academy Awards. She took to the stage in buckskin and adorned in traditional, flowing hair-ties. 'I'm Apache', she told the film-world dignitaries, and then announced that Brando was turning down the award in protest against the 'treatment of American Indians today by the film industry'. Boos erupted in the auditorium (something that would never happen at the Oscars today), and Littlefeather went down in cultural history as the Native American who stuck it to the Hollywood man.

Only, it was an act. Ironically. Following her death in October 2022, Littlefeather's family said they had no Native ancestry. '"Native American" Littlefeather who caused Oscar storm was a fraud, say sisters', as the stark headline in *The Times* put it.[9] She was not Apache, they said, but the daughter of a white woman and a Mexican man. Her birth name was Marie Louise Cruz. Our family has 'no tribal identity', the sisters said. 'It is a fraud', one of them said of Littlefeather's lifetime of Native posing. 'It's disgusting to the heritage of the tribal people.'[10]

There is something striking about the fact that the slamming of Hollywood for its unjust depictions of 'American Indians' came from someone who herself seems to have been mimicking an American Indian. An actor having a pop at actors. This now celebrated moment in Hollywood history – the Academy apologised to Littlefeather for the hostile reception she received in 1973 and held an event in her honour in September 2022 – was itself a little bit Hollywood, involving the donning of a costume and the performance of pain. Hollywood may have had a tendency to depict Native Americans as a strange and violent people, as the 'Indians' always taking on our 'Cowboys'. But in hamming it up as an Apache, as one of the maltreated ones of history, Littlefeather was also caricaturing Native Americans to make a cultural point about America. Not that those pesky Indians had thwarted Americans' gallant and daring Westward expansion of the 19th century, but that the expansion itself was the real problem, a kind of genocide, speaking to the base urges of the land-hungry white man.

The Brando / Littlefeather stunt was something of a turning point in the modern cultural ethos. It spoke to a shift from the cultural elite putting actors in American Indian dress to make a point about the goodness of America to the cultural elite putting *itself* in American Indian dress to make a point about the wickedness of America. From self-confidence to self-loathing. From the othering of indigenous people to the othering of America itself.

The problem isn't only Pretendians. Other forms of race fakery abound, too. Whites pretending to be black, for example. Everyone knows of the case of Rachel Dolezal, a chapter president for the National Association for the Advancement of Coloured People in the US who was exposed in 2015 as a white woman masquerading as black. Her tanned skin and fluffed-up fake afro were a cynical performance of blackness. Even following her exposure as the daughter of white folk of German, Czech and Swedish origin, and the discovery of childhood pics in which she is clearly a white girl with blue eyes and straight blonde hair, still Dolezal claimed blackness. 'I identify as black', she said in 2017. She might not be black but she *feels* black, and in her view that's enough, it makes her black.

There was also the case of Jessica Krug. This is the white, Kansas-born academic who pretended to be a woman of North African descent. Or sometimes a black woman of Caribbean descent who grew up in the Bronx. She liked to mix it up. She was an associate professor at George Washington University with an academic focus on Africa and the African diaspora. For years, she essentially blacked up – 'The white professor who posed as black', as one headline had it.[11] Even though she 'peddled gross caricatures' and 'fabricated harrowing personal backstories', it still took ages for anyone to see through her act. She said she'd been abandoned by her father as a child and that she had once been raped. She sometimes called herself Jess La Bombalera and claimed she was from the Bronx – or 'the hood'. She said her mother was Puerto Rican and a drug addict. She peppered her chat with the word 'Y'all' and frequently spoke in what one observer described as a 'D-list imitation Bronx accent'.[12] And still no questions were asked. For years. She just carried on at the prestigious George Washington University, teaching her courses on 'dismantling whiteness'.[13]

The truth, when it finally came out, was almost too ridiculous for words. Ms Krug, Ms La Bombalera from the hood, was actually white and Jewish and from Overland Park, an upper-middle-class, overwhelmingly white suburb of Kansas City. She had a bat mitzvah at 13. She went to some of the most esteemed private schools in Kansas, including one that counts the co-founder of Tinder and the former press secretary to Barack Obama, Josh Earnest, among its former students. The Bronx, the Puerto Rican junky mother, the almost comedic Latinx street accent – it was lie upon lie. Krug essentially adopted the most cartoon version of a tough-life ethnic-minority woman you could think of, and everyone fell for it. Everyone nodded along as this Latina minstrel passed off a pulp-fiction take on a brown woman's life as her own.

This trend of race fakery matters. These episodes of blacked-up pretension tell us something important about our times. They especially tell us something important about identity politics, that most divisive of creeds that increasingly reigns supreme in the public life of Anglo-America in the 21st century.

Critics of Pretendians and race fakers tend to focus on the financial gains these people make. Lori Campbell of the Indigenous Engagement Association at the University of Regina in Canada has spoken of the 'concerns within indigenous communities' that there are people out there 'who are fraudulently pretending to be indigenous in order to access resources and opportunities'.[14]

That's doubtless part of the race-scam trend. Certain academic and professional positions are indeed contingent on coming from the right racial background. Carrie Bourassa wouldn't have risen to be a director at the Institute of Indigenous Peoples' Health had she not managed to spin the swindle about being Métis. The publishing world, meanwhile, is today far keener on the 'authentic' stories of people from ethnic-minority backgrounds, especially if those stories include a generous serving of racism and other social pains, than it is on seeing yet another novel from yet another white man. Joyce Carol Oates surely had a point when she said literary agents find it hard to 'get editors to read first novels by young white male writers, no matter how good'. 'They are just not interested', said Oates.[15] In a world where certain ethnic experiences are handsomely rewarded on campuses and in book deals, you can certainly earn a few more bucks if you put on a buckskin or swap your nice, middle-class Jewish-girl origins for the identity of a woman from the hood whose mum was on drugs.

But there's more going on here than money-grubbing. More pertinently, and more worryingly, the rise of race-faking speaks to the corrosive consequences of identity politics. It speaks to the extent to which this hyper-racialist ideology has reorganised the intellectual and social life of our nations. The way it has introduced new racial hierarchies that elevate some ethnic experiences as good, and worth aspiring to, and denigrate others as bad, and worth only discarding, as Krug and others discarded theirs. And it speaks to the deep urge to censure and silence in the identitarian ideology, so that even obvious pretenders, waving their Native feathers and speaking in their sub-'Jenny from the Block' accents, can continue their masquerade for years because no one dare question them, lest they be accused of giving offence, of negating someone's racial reality, of demeaning a 'lived experience'.

Consider the Krug case. There will be many reasons exclusive to Krug that she went about pretending to be the Afro-Latina daughter of a smackhead mother. That is not something that normal people do. But culturally there is an undeniable logic to her behaviour. As we've seen, we live in a time of anti-whiteness. Whiteness is treated as a marker for 'privilege', proof of a possibly toxic soul. Universities and workplaces overflow with schemes for 'healing' people of their whiteness and exorcising their 'internalised white supremacy'. Indeed, Krug made her big splash at George Washington University by talking about the importance of 'dismantling whiteness'.[16] That's where the cultural clout lies these days, that's where the moral authority lives: in being anti-white, in seeking to cleanse the world of the white pox.

In such a time, is it really surprising if someone like Krug goes a step further and seeks to fully, physically absolve herself of whiteness by pulling on the garb of an Afro-Latina woman instead? Krug is Jewish, too – another identity that enjoys little cultural validation in the new systems of racial hierarchy. Jews are seen as too privileged, too white. They're seen as part of the problem. We are steeped in a political culture that is hell-bent on curing whiteness; a culture that is uncomfortable with the Jews. Why wouldn't someone like Krug jettison her real life and fashion a fake one?

This was surely her ham-fisted attempt to escape the severe racial judgements of the identitarian era. Krug was doing, in a more extreme form, what many whites do today: express shame towards their heritage, and even seek to liberate themselves from that heritage. What is the practice of checking one's white privilege, for example, if not self-flagellation for the sin of whiteness?[17] Christopher Lasch noted, decades ago, the tendency of some whites to adopt the language, ideas and culture of 'the ghetto'. Consider the growing popularity of the term of abuse 'motherfucker', he said. It seemed to Lasch that whites had embraced 'the obscenity of the ghetto to convey a posture of militant alienation'.[18] He provocatively argued that 'the attraction of black culture for disaffected whites suggests that black culture now speaks to a *general condition*, the most important feature of which is a loss of faith in the future'.

This is what we have today, though in an even more pronounced form. Identity politics has intensified the disaffectedness of whites while simultaneously imbuing black culture with the highest moral status. The end result is a popular culture in which white has become a byword for lame and black a byword for cool. A world in which whites will kneel down and beg blacks for forgiveness. In which students and workers alike are invited to undergo training to make them reckon with their whiteness or even to make them 'less white'.[19]

Isn't that what Krug and Dolezal and Bourassa and all the other race fakers were aiming for – to be less white? Sure, the mainstream political culture only expects people to be 'less white' by checking their privilege and acknowledging black pain, whereas the race fakers became 'less white' by overdoing the fake tan, adopting hammy urban accents and waving around tribal feathers; by lying. But the aim in all cases was the same: less whiteness. Krug and Co only did with more vim what our identity society demands of us all – eschew your bad identity and learn about better, purer ones.

Aren't we all pretenders now, at some level? Different forms of 'race fakery' can be seen everywhere. Among white youths who speak in black patois; who seem to prefer the sensation of black alienation to their own apparently 'lame' white lives. Among middle-class white women who adorn themselves in the paraphernalia of exotic Eastern imagery, whether that's Tibetan Buddhism or Indian spiritualism. Is that not just a more polite, 'normal' version of the identity pantomimes engaged in by the likes of Jessica Krug?

We might also argue that the new generation that obsessively cultivates identities of queerness – genderqueer, queer-curious, pansexual – is engaging in a sexual version of race fakery. Here the aim is not to escape the uncelebrated identity of whiteness but the curse of being heterosexual – that square, archaic, biology-based lifestyle that no switched-on young person wants. Between 2017 and 2021, the proportion of American youths in Generation Z who identify as LGBTQ rose from 10.5 per cent to 20.8 per cent. In the UK, eight per cent of those aged 16 to 24 identify as LGBTQ, compared with just one per cent of people over the age of 65.[20] We used to have gay shame, do we now have straight shame? The young fleeing their boring heterosexuality? Where Dolezal bouffants her pseudo-afro and tops up the spray-tan, they dye their hair pink or blue and pull on the fashion uniform of the sexually curious. I'm not white, I'm not straight, I'm not *problematic* – these are the desperate cries of both blatant fakers and subtle fakers in our unforgiving era of identity.

This is not an argument against so-called cultural appropriation. The woke obsession with 'cultural appropriation', with reprimanding those who drift from their own supposed racial lane into someone else's, is reactionary and illiberal. It speaks to that ossification of race we've already discussed; to the backward idea that blacks and whites are different, and will be forever, and thus relations between them must be strictly policed and controlled. There is nothing whatsoever wrong with white youths loving black culture, or with black people engaging in what our elites wrongly describe as 'white culture', whether that's Beethoven's Fifth or the Shakespeare plays. The race of an artist or entertainer should count for nought. All of us, armed with that universal human urge to discover and learn, should move freely through the Kingdom of Culture, with no regard for either woke or reactionary decrees about what 'our culture' should consist of.

No, the issue is that much of today's dabbling in supposedly more authentic identities is clearly driven by a crisis of identity; by a discomfort with the self; by a feeling that one's own identity is deficient in some way. Too white, too straight, too dull – that is often the starting-point feeling among those who engage in forms of identity experimentation that sometimes cross the line into identity fakery. This is the true problem with identity politics in the 21st century: the way it delegitimises certain identities and the inevitable consequence this has of sowing self-doubt and even self-loathing among those cursed with one of the 'problematic' identities.

This is the thing: identity politics doesn't only celebrate identities – it denigrates identities, too. Identity delegitimation is central to the identitarian cause. Through this process, the individual, especially the white, straight, male individual, is violently torn from his own nationality, his own historical origins, even his own sexuality. He's encouraged to feel shame towards his identity. So maybe find a new one? One a little less male, a little less straight, a little less white? We arrive in the era of the Great Pretender, where people fake it. Where instead of *being*, they perform. Where instead of *knowing* who they are, they ask others to tell them who they are. Where instead of *living*, they search, always, endlessly, for some new costume or role that might secure for them a little more affirmation from the identitarian elites. This is identity politics' most unforgivable sin – its wresting of the individual from himself, from his truth, and its demand that he apologise for what he is or become something else entirely. Identitarianism makes fakers of us all.

For me, the most striking phrase of the identity era is the one that was uttered by Rachel Dolezal when she was outed as white: 'I identify as black.' *I identify as*… There it is. The *cri de coeur* of our times. Nothing speaks more profoundly to the crisis of identity than that phrase, 'I identify as…'. In the past, we were. You didn't identify as something, you just were that thing. 'I am a shoemaker'. 'I am a mother.' 'I am a Catholic.' 'I am a humanist.' 'I am a man.' There was a confidence, a certainty, to people's sense of identity, and to their declarations of that identity.

Today, instead of being something, people identify as something. 'I identify as working class.' 'I identify as a Marxist.' 'I identify as queer.' 'I identify as a woman.' (That one is as frequently uttered by men as by women. More so, in fact. Most women still say 'I'm a woman'. It's men in the grip of identitarian gender play who are more likely to say, 'I identify as a woman'.) And Dolezal's infamous cry: 'I identify as black.' She can't say 'I am black' – concrete reality still counts for something, if not much, in our relativistic times. But she can identify as black. She can engage in the great pretence.

The rise and rise of 'I identify as…', the ascendancy of self-identification, is one of the most notable developments in this young century. It speaks to a shift from being to passing through. From a clear sense of presence in the world to a feeling of transience. From identities that were rooted and real, to identities that seem tentative, insecure, questionable. Those three words, 'I identify as…', feel strikingly contingent. They give voice to a sense of flux and changeability. 'I identify as such-and-such for now' is the undertone of this most curious of modern declarations.

Indeed, these highly personalised 'identifications as' often come with the acknowledgement that the identification might change over time, and change dramatically. So one non-binary activist tells us that he (she? they?) 'identifies as both genders' for now, but 'I do not know who I will be, where I am going or whom I will identify as in the future.'[21] *I do not know who I will be* – this is the unanchoring and bewilderment of our times summed up.

Changeability is built into some of the new identities. You can be one thing one day, something else the next. The *Daily Mail* reported on the case of a trans person who flits from male to female. One day he / she / they 'wakes up and chooses to wear a dress and heels to work, while others she's a man and dons baggy jeans and workmen boots'.[22] There was also the story of the businessman – or businessthey – who identifies as a man on some days (Philip) and as a woman on other days (Pippa). He – reason forces me to describe his actual sex rather than his fantasised genders – even won a woman-in-business award, but presumably only for those days on which he 'wears wigs and dresses'.[23]

The contingency of the cult of self-ID is clear from the burgeoning phrase 'I *currently* identify as…'. There is a veritable universe of online chat involving people who currently identify as something, with the use of that word, 'currently', strongly hinting that they might not identify as that thing for very long. Perhaps they'll switch, from one sex to another, like Philip / Pippa, or from one class to another, or from one race to another, like Dolezal. Or maybe even from one species to another. On the outskirts of identitarianism, the rise of pup play and of neopronouns like kitten / kittenself speak to an urge to opt out of humanity itself. 'Being human is so last year, the next frontier is trans-speciesism', says the *Evening Standard*. 'There are plenty of people out there who suffer from species dysphoria these days', apparently. 'They feel they are a non-human species trapped in a human body.'[24]

This makes messed-up sense. If ashamed whites can self-identify as black, and ashamed straights can self-identify as genderqueer, why shouldn't ashamed human beings, appalled by human behaviour and the human impact on the planet, identify as beasts? If you can identify out of your race, sex and sexuality, surely you can identify out of your humanity, too. Self-identification as post-human, post-that-pox-on-Earth – it's coming.

There's a meme doing the rounds that says '"I identify as" means "I pretend to be"'. There's some truth in this. The Pretendians, and others, really are pretending. But we should not be too cynical about self-ID. It is not as conscious a stance as some make out. Rather, it reflects the very real thinness and subjectivity of human identity today. The replacement of 'I am' with 'I identify as' tells an important story about the obliteration of the bonds between a person's experiences and his identity.

The truly striking thing about the times we live in is not so much the obsession with identity as the instability of identity. Wanting an identity is not a problem. How could it be? We all want to be something, whether we define ourselves by what we do, what we believe, or what we are. The desire to define oneself, and thus to project oneself on to the world, is a positive one. The working-class identity, the female identity, the radical identity – all have played a key role in recent decades in shaking up, for the better, society's priorities and principles.

Those identities were real, though. They were informed and shaped by experience and work and belief. Today, identity seems unreal. Identity is no longer an extension or an expression of our lives. Rather, it is something you can choose, ideally from a preordained list of good identities. It is a thing we chop and change in accordance with the political fashion. It is something we take our cues on from the guardians of right thinking and the thought-shapers of social media. Identity has been untethered from life and instead has become a costume – and you had better pick the right costume. This is the problem with identity politics: not the search for identity, but the dislocation of identity from one's own life.

This dislocation gives rise to a ridiculous world in which people can 'identify as' almost anything they like, even if it bears no resemblance to reality. Like Dolezal pretending to be black. Or Krug making out she's a survivor from 'the hood'. Or the 53-year-old Norwegian man who now identifies not only as a woman, but also as disabled. He feels, he says, that he 'should have been paralysed from the waist down'.[25]

But the more important crisis here is the corrosion of real, meaningful identities. All the things people might once have identified themselves through – nation, church, work, family – have been hugely hollowed out. The world of work has been thoroughly disorganised. Traditional 'male' jobs are out and a softer, more 'feminised' workplace is in, with short-term contracts and job-sharing ruling the day. Trade-union membership has stagnated. Industrial action, give or take some big strikes here and there, has dissipated.

Religion has ebbed, too. In the UK, church membership fell from 10.6million in 1930 to 5.5million in 2010. By 2013, it had fallen to 5.4million. Percentage-wise, this represents a collapse in regular church-goers from 30 per cent of the population in 1930 to just over 10 per cent in 2013. As for family life, the relentless intervention of nanny statists into the home, the onward march of specialised expertise even into the realm of parenting, has had the inexorable impact of denuding the identities of mother and father of their truth and independence. It's turned mother and father into 'parents' who must be furnished by officialdom with the 'skills' they need to raise their kids.[26]

It is this evacuation of substance from our old identities that inflames the frantic hunt for new identities, for something, *anything*, by which we might define ourselves. Absent the workplace identity, the social identity, the family identity, and under instruction from the elites to feel shame about our national or cultural identities, more and more people feel lost, uncertain, identity-less.

This matters. It matters for people's sense of self, and it matters for liberty, too. Identity politics stokes a culture of unknowing. Unknow yourself, be unsure of yourself, trust others instead to determine which identities are good and which are bad – that is what the cult of identitarianism tells us. The beginning of Western philosophy, the beginning of Western civilisation itself, is embodied in the cry, 'Know thyself'. That piece of Ancient Greek philosophical advice that echoes down the ages was designed to encourage self-awareness, 'a search for self-understanding', as one modern account has it.[27] It was reportedly carved into stone at the entrance to Apollo's Temple in Delphi in Greece, such was the importance of this most human of ideals.

Identity politics, in stark, depressing contrast, encourages a lack of knowing; a separation of the self from the self so profound that we require external forces to intervene and decree which of our experiences are bad, and thus deserving of erasure, and which are good, and thus deserving of embrace. Identitarianism represents not only a negation of the enlightened post-racial politics of late 20th-century liberalism, but also of that Ancient cry that we can and *must* know ourselves.

In place of 'Know thyself' we have 'Let us tell you who you should be'. We are continually instructed on the correct way to think, speak, be. Rid yourself of that problematic identity and adopt this one instead, say our identitarian overlords. Kant had the answer to such presumptive efforts to control our lives. In his 1784 essay, 'What is Enlightenment?', he raged against those who would tell us what to think and how to exist. He complained of having 'a book that thinks for me, a pastor who acts as my conscience, a physician who prescribes my diet', all of which means 'I have no need to exert myself'. These 'guardians', he said, treat us like 'cattle', making us view 'the step to maturity not only as hard, but also as extremely dangerous'. The solution to such harmful meddling? Ignore it. 'Walk firmly' and 'cultivate your own mind', said Kant.[28] *'Have the courage to use your own understanding.'*

So it must be today, too. Remember, you will always know yourself better than they know you.

1 Activist makes list to bust imposters claiming to be Native American, *New York Post*, 1 January 2022

2 Canadian health expert who claimed to be 'Morning Star Bear' steps aside after Indigenous ancestry questioned, *Washington Post*, 2 November 2021

3 Canadian health expert who claimed to be 'Morning Star Bear' steps aside after Indigenous ancestry questioned, *Washington Post*, 2 November 2021

4 How disgraced health expert Carrie Bourassa passed as indigenous for years, *New York Post*, 1 December 2021

5 How disgraced health expert Carrie Bourassa passed as indigenous for years, *New York Post*, 1 December 2021

6 Author Joseph Boyden's shape-shifting Indigenous identity, *APTN*, 23 December 2016

7 Author Joseph Boyden's shape-shifting Indigenous identity, *APTN*, 23 December 2016

8 Joseph Boyden's Apology and the Strange History of 'Pretendians', *Vice*, 12 January 2017

9 'Native American' Littlefeather who caused Oscar storm was a fraud, say sisters, *The Times*, 24 October 2022

10 Sacheen Littlefeather Lied About Native American Ancestry, Sisters Claim, *Rolling Stone*, 22 October 2022

11 The True Story of Jess Krug, the White Professor Who Posed as Black for Years – Until It All Blew Up Last Fall, *Washingtonian*, 27 January 2021

12 The True Story of Jess Krug, the White Professor Who Posed as Black for Years – Until It All Blew Up Last Fall, *Washingtonian*, 27 January 2021

13 Jessica Krug and the fakeness of identity politics, Brendan O'Neill, *spiked*, 7 September 2020

14 Saskatchewan experts weigh in following release of Indigenous Identity Fraud report, *Global News*, 4 November 2022

15 Oates Tweets About 'Young White Male Writers', *Kirkus*, 25 July 2022

16 Jessica Krug and the fakeness of identity politics, Brendan O'Neill, *spiked*, 7 September 2020

17 Check yourself: the White Privilege Test, European University Institute, monitorracism.eu

18 *Culture of Narcissism: American Life in an Age of Diminishing Expectations*, Christopher Lasch, WW Norton (1979)

19 Coca-Cola slammed for diversity training that urged workers to be 'less white', *New York Post*, 23 February 2021

20 Is Harry Styles ashamed of being straight?, Brendan O'Neill, *Spectator*, 24 August 2022

21 11 Times Gender Norms Got The Middle Finger in 2015, MTV, 7 December 2015

22 I've got no control on whether I'm going to be Layton or Layla: Bi-gender teenager lives life as a man and a woman ... wearing baggy jeans or revealing dresses, *Daily Mail*, 21 January 2015

23 You can NEVER be our woman of the year! City workers hit out at genderfluid banker who works some days as Philip and others as Pippa, *Daily Mail*, 23 September 2018

24 Being human is so last year, the next frontier is trans-speciesism according to these new books, *Evening Standard*, 19 April 2016

25 Norwegian Man Now Identifies as a Disabled Woman, Uses Wheelchair 'Almost All The Time', *Reduxx*, 1 November 2022

26 Parenting Skills Are A Con, Frank Furedi, *Huffington Post*, 31 May 2013

27 Know Thyself: The Philosophy of Self-Knowledge, *Uconn Today*, 7 August 2018

28 *An Answer to the Question: What is Enlightenment?*, Immanuel Kant, Penguin Great Ideas (2009)

10

WORDS WOUND

Words hurt, they say. This is the ideological underpinning to so much censorship today – the idea that words wound, as a punch might wound. The imagery of violence is deployed in almost every call for censure in the 21st-century West. Speech has been reimagined as aggression, hence 'microaggressions'. People speak of feeling 'assaulted' by speech. 'Words, like sticks and stones, can assault; they can injure; they can exclude' – that's the thesis of *Words That Wound*, an influential tome published in 1993.[1] Activists claim to feel 'erased' by controversial or disagreeable utterances. Trans campaigners speak darkly of 'trans erasure', as if words from the other side of the divide, the speech of gender-critical feminists, might contain that most awesome and nullifying power of genocide.

Words make us feel 'unsafe', people say. Witness the rise and rise of Safe Spaces on university campuses, designed to ensure students' psychic security against the terrible threat of their hearing an idea they disagree with. Safe Spaces recreate the state of childhood, complete with colouring books and ice cream, speaking to how determinedly some long to retreat from the adult world of hurtful chatter and brickbats.[2]

The United Nations wrings its hands over 'hate speech and *real harm*' (my emphasis). The 'weaponisation of public discourse for political gain' can lead to 'stigmatisation, discrimination and large-scale violence', it says.[3] Better keep a check on those hurtful words. One US university even maintains a list of 'words that hurt'. It includes the phrase 'You guys'.[4] That scandalous utterance 'erases the identities of people who are in the room' and 'generalise[s] a group of people to be masculine'. Shut it down. Silence that act of violence.

Both the formal and informal punishment of words rests on the belief that they can wound. Laws in Europe claim to guard people from speech that is alarming, distressing, hurtful. The overlords of social media censor speech for 'the wellbeing of our community'.[5] Everywhere the cry goes up: words injure, they can cut like a knife, they can be used as 'weapons to ambush, terrorise, wound, humiliate and degrade'.[6] And just as the law protects us from such dreadful things when they are done to our bodies with fists and kicks, surely it should also protect us from them when they are done to our minds with words and ideas. Surely our psychic wellbeing should be accorded as much respect by the powers-that-be as our physical integrity is.

The temptation of many of us who believe in freedom of speech, in the liberty of all to utter their beliefs and ideas, is to damn this claim that 'words hurt' as a libel against public discourse. As a slippery untruth that is cynically designed to depict words as all-powerful, as containing so much energy, so much heat, that they can lay waste to self-esteem and even make us fret over erasure, over being wiped out entirely by that sore comment or that disturbing idea. Actually, we often say, words are just words. They're not sticks, they're not stones, they're *words*. They won't kill you, they won't hurt you, you'll be fine. They say words are a force of nature like no other, we say: 'Relax. It's just speech.'

We need to stop doing this. We need to stop countering the new censors by accusing them of exaggerating the power and the potency of words. We need to stop responding to their painting of speech as a dangerous, disorientating force by defensively pleading that words don't wound because they're just words. We need to stop reacting to their branding of speech as a weapon, as a tool of ambush and degradation, by effectively draining speech of its power and saying: 'It's only speech.' As if speech were a small thing, almost an insignificant thing, more likely to contain calming qualities than upsetting ones, more likely to help us overcome conflict rather than stir it up, more likely to offer a balm to your soul than to stab at it as a knife might stab at your body.

For when we do this, we play down the power of words. And that includes the power of words to wound. Words do wound. It's true. Words hurt people, they hurt institutions, they hurt belief systems. Words make churches tremble and ideologies quake. Words inflict pain on priests and princes and ideologues. Words upend the social order. Words rip away the comforting ideas people and communities might have wrapped themselves in for decades, centuries perhaps. Words ambush the complacent and degrade the powerful. Words cause discord, angst, even conflict. Isn't every revolution in history the offspring of words? Of *ideas*? Words do destabilise, they do disorientate. People are right to sometimes feel afraid of words. Words are dangerous. When they say words wound, we should say: 'I agree.'

But here's the thing: it is precisely because words can wound, precisely because of their power to unsettle, that they should never be restricted. It is precisely the unpredictable energy and influence of speech that means it must be put beyond the jurisdiction of all earthly authorities. Because nothing that empowers the individual to such an extent that it allows him to sow and spread ideas that might one day change society for the better should ever be constricted. They say the power of speech justifies its censure and control. We should say the opposite: the fact that speech is powerful is all the justification we need to let it be free, everywhere and always.

We must point out that where words hurt – and they do – censorship hurts more. Physically, spiritually, existentially, censorship is more wounding to the individual, and to society, than unfettered speech is. Those in the 21st century who claim to feel bruised and bloodied by words should take some time to read up on the heretics of history, and even the heretics of today. You want to see wounding? Witness their trials.

Consider William Tyndale (1494–1536), one of the great heretics in the history of England. Tyndale was a 16th-century religious scholar who would become a leading light in the Protestant Reformation. His crime, his utterance of words that hurt, was to translate the Bible into English. That was forbidden at the time. Biblical knowledge was for priests only, for men versed in Latin, for men of learning and insight, not for the English-speaking throng. As FL Clarke put it in his great 19th-century biography, *The Life of William Tyndale*, 'good and noble' men thought that 'for the Bible to be placed in the hands of the common people was a dangerous thing – the poor and ignorant should be content to hear only those portions that the priests might think fit to read in the churches; *they* were the shepherds who were appointed to feed the sheep'.[7]

Tyndale disagreed. And he was willing to risk life and limb for this disagreement. He made it his life's work to translate, print and distribute the Bible. Forbidden from doing so in England, he travelled to Germany, where Luther's translation of the New Testament into German had appeared in 1522. Tyndale's translation of the New Testament went to print in Cologne in 1525. But his continual hunting by agents of the English Crown and the Catholic Church – he was 'hunted like an outlaw', always 'working clandestinely' – forced him on to the run.[8] He moved further south in Germany, to work with another printer, where he published a pocket edition of the Bible. This is how that thing we take for granted today – a carriable, readable version of the Bible in one's own tongue – was created. Tyndale's Bibles were smuggled on ships to England, hidden in cargos of grain and among other merchandise, ready to be spirited among the people by his sympathisers. The Bibles were 'copied in secret and read in terror', says Clarke.

It is difficult to overstate Tyndale's contribution to freedom of conscience and freedom of speech. In translating and printing and spreading the Bible, Tyndale was doing more than challenging the stranglehold that the Catholic Church had over religious ideas, over the Word of God itself. He was also, in turn, expressing a great faith in ordinary people's ability to understand things for themselves. To no longer require 'shepherds' to instruct them and guide their thoughts. His trust was not only in God, but also in the capacity of 'the ignorant and the unlearned' to enlighten themselves.[9] It was a searingly radical idea. It *remains* a radical idea, still unfulfilled in so many ways.

No, we are no longer deprived of English-language Bibles. But we are discouraged from reading certain texts, lest they unsettle or inflame our small minds. 'Is it a book that you would even wish your wife or servants to read?', as the prosecutor in the *Lady Chatterley's Lover* trial of 1960 infamously asked.[10] Today good and noble people still believe that for certain books 'to be placed in the hands of the common people [is] a dangerous thing'. Only now they don't crush or pulp said books, as the ecclesiastical authorities did with Tyndale's Bibles, but rather add trigger warnings to them. That's the new form of shepherding, where experts, rather than priests, attach danger signs to books so that we sheep will know of the risk involved in reading them, and might avoid reading them entirely.

The other idea – the heretical idea – that people should be free to read and see for themselves was one Tyndale was willing to die for. He was condemned as a heretic by Cardinal Wolsey in 1529. The authorities eventually caught up with the Bible-translating outlaw and he was arrested in 1535 and transported to Vilvoorde Castle near Brussels. The next year he was convicted of heresy. He was strangled to death in public and then burnt at the stake so that 'the mortal remains of William Tyndale were an indistinguishable heap of ashes!'.[11] Words hurt? They do. But not nearly as much as strangulation and fire. Censorship is infinitely more violent than freedom.

Or consider another great heretic of old, John Lilburne (1614–1657). Lilburne was a political agitator. He was a Leveller during, and after, the English Civil War – that portion of the rebels that believed in a greater expansion of democratic rights than Cromwell was willing to concede. Lilburne coined the term 'freeborn rights' to describe the fundamental liberties we all just have, or ought to have. The liberty to think and speak for ourselves and to choose who should govern us.

The idea of representative democracy spread through England like a fire in the 1640s, largely thanks to the 'blizzard of gloriously intemperate pamphlets from the pen of John Lilburne'.[12] Lilburne raged against the menace of undemocratic, unaccountable rule. 'Unnatural, irrational, sinful, wicked, unjust, devilish and tyrannical it is', he wrote, 'for any man whatsoever – spiritual or temporal, clergyman or layman – to appropriate and assume unto himself a power, authority and jurisdiction to rule, govern or reign over any sort of men in the world without their free consent'. This remains a radical idea, too. Also unfulfilled. To see that, one need only observe the furious reaction of the elites to the swinish multitude's rejection of the European Union in the 2016 referendum, which was a rejection of the idea that commissions in Brussels should have the right to draw up our laws despite not having our free consent to do so.

Prior to the English Civil War, Lilburne, then young and not well-known, had shown himself as willing as Tyndale had been a century earlier to suffer for his beliefs. In the mid-1630s, William Prynne, the Puritan controversialist, wrote a pamphlet titled *News From Ipswich*, in which he slammed a particularly intolerant and regressive bishop and took aim at the Star Chamber, too – the institution of royal control over public printing. For this, he was himself dragged before the Star Chamber in 1637 and charged with seditious libel. He was fined, publicly whipped, put in the pillory, had the tops of his ears cut off, and his cheeks were branded with the letters 'S' and 'L' for seditious libel.[13]

Lilburne, then an apprentice in London in his early twenties, was horrified by the torture of Prynne. He also shared Prynne's criticisms of the bishops. He had helped to spirit Prynne's tracts, and others, into England to distribute them among the people. Young Lilburne was himself taken to the Star Chamber and found guilty of smuggling blasphemous materials and condemned to whipping. He was 'tied to the back of a cart on a hot summer's day and unremittingly whipped as he walked with a bare back all the way from the eastern end of Fleet Street to Westminster Palace Yard'. One bystander guessed Lilburne had received 500 blows from the whip. His shoulders 'swelled almost as big as a penny loafe with the bruses of the knotted Cords'.[14]

Most strikingly, Lilburne just wouldn't shut up. When he arrived at the pillory in Westminster, 'in spite of his wounds and the burning sunshine', he loudly told his story and reiterated his criticisms of the bishops. The radical crowd lapped it up. A lawyer told him to shut up, but he wouldn't. So he was gagged, 'so roughly that blood spurted from his mouth', but even that didn't do the trick. Lilburne took copies of dissident pamphlets from his pockets and threw them among the people. After that, his mouth gagged and his pamphlets all gone, and with no other means of expression left to him, he 'stamped his feet until the two hours were up'.[15] A good heretic never falls silent, in any circumstance.

So, yes, words hurt. But not as much as receiving 500 lashes and a bloodied gob for the crime of expressing dissident thoughts, of using your speech to 'hurt' authority.

Or let us fast forward 400 years to some heretics of today. The good people of *Charlie Hebdo*. Their offence is well known – they mocked Muhammad. (And other religious leaders, too.) And for that they paid the ultimate price, the same price as Tyndale: execution; death for heresy.

No, the slaughter of 10 writers and cartoonists at the *Charlie Hebdo* offices in January 2015 was not officially sanctioned, as was Tyndale's strangulation and Lilburne's public torture. But it can be viewed as a violent expression of an official *idea* – namely, that it is wrong to give offence, including to Islam.

Indeed, France is a country in which you can be taken to court for calling Islam 'the stupidest religion', as novelist Michel Houellebecq was in 2002 (he was acquitted).[16] It's a country in which you can be fined thousands of euros for demeaning Islam, for saying that Muslims are 'destroying our country by imposing their ways', as Brigitte Bardot was in 2008 (and on other occasions, too).[17] Saïd and Chérif Kouachi, the radical Islamist brothers who visited that barbarism upon *Charlie Hebdo*, did not have to look to the Koran or to the statements of Eastern imams to fortify their belief that criticism of their religion is wrong and *punishable*. That was a belief written into the very laws of the land in which they were born and brought up. Their atrocity can be seen as the militant wing of political correctness, an extrajudicial enforcement of the heresy-hunting that is a central feature of governance and control in the West today.

So, yes, words can be painful. They can be used as weapons. You can feel 'ambushed, terrorised and wounded' by them. But that pain is incomparable to the pain of the physical ambush of the *Charlie Hebdo* offices, and the pain of the grief and sorrow those 10 deaths will have caused. *Charlie Hebdo* is accused of 'punching down'. That metaphor of violence – punching – should induce shame in everyone who uses it given the real, barbaric violence the *Charlie Hebdo* staff suffered for their blasphemies. The barbarism of censorship outweighs the pain of words, every time.

There are other ways censorship hurts us, and society, more than speech does. Censorship dulls our critical senses. It infantilises us by imploring us to trust others to decide on our behalf what we should think about the world. It implicitly instructs us to suspend thought and analysis and instead let the wisdom of the more learned, of today's secular shepherds, wash over us. Censorship is an invitation to revert to a childlike state, which makes it unsurprising that modern zones of censorship – Safe Spaces – so often resemble kindergartens for adults. Those spaces are a real, physical manifestation of the childish nature censorship asks us all to embrace.

Censorship nurtures rigid thinking, too. When we hide ourselves and our ideas from contestation, debate, mockery and rebuke, our minds become ossified. We start to believe what we believe not because we have tested it against the doubts and disagreements of others, but because we just know it is right. This is how an idea becomes a catechism, how a political movement becomes a religion, how an individual turns from a free thinker into the imperious holder of what he presumes to be perfect, untouchable, unquestionable beliefs. Censorship is the handmaiden of dogmatism. Freedom, in contrast, is the implacable foe of dogmatism.

John Stuart Mill knew the dangers of protecting ideas from challenge. Your every effort to silence speech is an 'assumption of infallibility', he said. There is only one way to know if we are right about something, said Mill, and that is by submitting our beliefs to the severe test of public opinion and public dissent. 'Complete liberty of contradicting and disproving our opinion, is the very condition which justifies us in assuming its truth for purposes of action; and on no other terms can a being with human faculties have any rational assurance of being right', he wrote.[18] Assuming rightness in the absence of freedom is how petty tyrants behave, all the way from those good and noble men who wanted to destroy Tyndale's dangerous Bibles to today's radical No Platforming of any thinker, politician or feminist whose heretical utterances threaten to expose or upend the new religions, the new ideologies.

And yet even as we remind people of the violence and intolerance of censorship, of censorship's threat to life as well as to our right to use our faculties of reason, we should not baulk from admitting that speech can be dangerous, too. Speech hurts. Very often it is intended to. That is one of its powers. Indeed, the heretics mentioned above knew very well that their speech was hurtful, that it would feel deeply unsettling and even threatening to many who heard it, and yet they continued to speak. They used their words as weapons.

Tyndale's idea of an English Bible was genuinely terrifying to the ecclesiastical order of the time and to those who adhered to that order. Tyndale's Bible will have felt as wounding to the Catholic zealots who threw it into the flames as a Germaine Greer article describing trans women as a 'gross parody of my sex' feels to many activists today.[19]

Lilburne positively revelled in the hurtfulness of his words to the priests and politicians who encountered them. No timid, cautious 'civil dialogue' for him – instead, he unleashed that 'blizzard of gloriously intemperate pamphlets'. Glorious intemperance is a virtue that defenders of free speech might be wise to resurrect. One historical account notes that Lilburne wielded both 'his pen and sword' with 'uncommon perseverance'. He 'possessed an unconquerable spirit' and was 'of so quarrelsome a disposition that it has been appositely said of him, that if there were none living but him, John would be against Lilburne, and Lilburne against John'.[20] There will have been few apologies from Lilburne for causing offence, few denials that words can indeed hurt, especially his words.

As for *Charlie Hebdo*, the most admirable thing about that magazine is its willingness to offend, to hurt. Just a few days after the massacre it was back to depicting Muhammad, this time holding a 'Je suis Charlie' sign with a tear running down his face. *Charlie* hurts not for the sake of it, but as a revolt against the stifling strictures against hurt, against the idea that there is no greater crime than to utter words that might make someone, or some religion, feel bad. To paraphrase Mill's argument that eccentricity becomes the duty of the free thinker in times of tyranny, we might also say that causing 'pain' is a moral obligation in an era in which stopping pain is so often the cynical justification for social control and censorship.

Too often today, believers in the liberty to speak baulk at the truth about words: they hurt. No, they are not violence – equating speech with violence is foolish and wrong. But speech is powerful, it can wound, it can induce pain in some of those who hear it. If speech did not have this power – to unsettle, to overthrow, to change minds and worlds radically – what would be the point of defending it? Surely we defend speech precisely because it contains so much extraordinary energy, because it can be a 'blizzard', because it *does* wound.

Some defenders of free speech end up, no doubt unwittingly, playing the same game as their opponents, by arguing that the heat and fury does indeed have to be drained from society every now and then. Only they think free speech is a better tool for achieving that draining than censorship. Where the censors insist that social control is necessary to maintain civility and calmness, the more liberal voices say that free civil dialogue makes a better fist of that task. There is nothing at all wrong with 'civil dialogue', of course. But it is a concept that will likely have been alien to Lilburne, and which would no doubt invoke scoffing at *Charlie Hebdo*. It seems to suggest that free speech is good because it pacifies, it tempers, it *calms*, when sometimes free speech is good because it does the opposite of all that. It fucks things up.

As one columnist argues, civility is 'the biggest weasel word of all'. '[W]ords like "respect" and "civility" [are used] to mark the boundaries of free speech', he says. So on some campuses, free speech is defended, but in the name of civil dialogue, and the consequence is not that different to when free speech is controlled in the name of avoiding harm or offence – that is, colour and daring are discouraged, in preference for the soothing hug of free civility, or therapeutic censure.[21] But freedom of speech is not social work. One is reminded of the words of French film director Claire Denis when she was challenged for not being politically correct in her films: 'What the fuck? I'm not a social worker.'[22]

We forget the hurtful, wild, unruly nature of unfettered speech at our peril. Societies have fallen as a result of free speech. Churches, too. Ideas that people felt they could not live without, whose destruction they felt would propel them into sorrow and chaos, have been wiped out by free speech. Heresy hurts. It is meant to. As Frederick Douglass said of freedom of speech, it is 'the dread of tyrants', for 'they know its power'. *'Thrones, dominions, principalities and powers, founded in injustice and wrong, are sure to tremble, if men are allowed to reason of righteousness, temperance, and of a judgement to come in their presence.'*[23]

Make them tremble – that, often, is what the heretic must do. So let's do it.

1 *Words That Wound: Critical Race Theory, Assaultive Speech, and the First Amendment*, Mari J Matsuda *et al.*, Routledge (1993)

2 Break out the Crayons and Play Doh on college campuses. College students need safe space, NC Spin, 30 January 2020

3 Hate speech and real harm, un.org

4 University of California Davis is suggesting students say 'y'all' to avoid offending people, *Business Insider*, 11 August 2016

5 TikTok bans misgendering, deadnaming from its content, NPR, 9 February 2022

6 *Words That Wound: Critical Race Theory, Assaultive Speech, and the First Amendment*, Mari J Matsuda *et al.*, Routledge (1993)

7 *The Life of William Tyndale*, FL Clarke, Leopold Classic Library (2015)

8 Freedom of Conscience, *Liberty Magazine*, January / February 2019

9 *The Life of William Tyndale*, FL Clarke, Leopold Classic Library (2015)

10 Would You Let Your Servant Read This Book?, *JSTOR Daily*, 15 November 2021

11 *The Life of William Tyndale*, FL Clarke, Leopold Classic Library (2015)

12 Up with the swinish multitude, Francis Wheen, *Guardian*, 26 February 2005

13 William Prynne, The Honourable Society of Lincoln's Inn, 27 June 2018

14 Courage and free speech, Timothy Garton Ash, *Aeon*, 29 September 2016

15 Courage and free speech, Timothy Garton Ash, *Aeon*, 29 September 2016

16 Houellebecq acquitted of insulting Islam, *Guardian*, 22 October 2002

17 Bardot fined over racial hatred, BBC News, 3 June 2008

18 *On Liberty and the Subjection of Women*, John Stuart Mill, Penguin Classics (2006)

19 On why sex change is a lie, Germaine Greer, *Independent*, 22 July 1989

20 *The Denham Tracts, Vol. 1: A Collection of Folklore, Reprinted From the Original Tracts and Pamphlets Printed by Denham Between 1846 and 1859*, Michael Aislabie Denham, Forgotten Books (2018)

21 Free speech, 'civility', and how universities are getting them mixed up, Michael Hiltzik, *Los Angeles Times*, 9 September 2014

22 Claire Denis on working with Robert Pattinson and navigating *High Life*'s deep space, AV Club, 17 April 2019

23 A plea for free speech in Boston, Frederick Douglass, 1860

About spiked

spiked is the magazine that wants to change the world as well as report on it. Edited by Tom Slater, and launched in 2001, it is irreverent where others conform, questioning where others wallow in received wisdom, and radical where others cling to the status quo.

At a time when it is fashionable to cancel 'problematic' people, to sideline voters when they give the 'wrong' answer, and to treat human beings as a drain on the planet, we put the case for human endeavour, the expansion of democracy, and freedom of speech with no ifs or buts.

Our motto is 'question everything' – or as the *New York Times* put it, we are 'the often-biting British publication fond of puncturing all manner of ideological balloons'.

Read us every day at spiked-online.com

About the author

Brendan O'Neill is the chief political writer for *spiked*, based in London. He was *spiked*'s editor for almost 15 years, from 2007 to 2021. He hosts the weekly podcast, *The Brendan O'Neill Show*. His writing has appeared in the *Spectator*, the *Sun*, the *Daily Mail* and the *Australian*. His previous collections of essays include *A Duty to Offend* and *Anti-Woke*.